EVERYTHING
YOU WANTED TO KNOW
ABOUT THE CATHOLIC CHURCH
BUT WERE TOO PIOUS TO ASK

the text of this book is printed
on 100% recycled paper

EVERYTHING
YOU WANTED TO KNOW
ABOUT THE CATHOLIC CHURCH
BUT WERE TOO PIOUS TO ASK

BY
ANDREW M. GREELEY

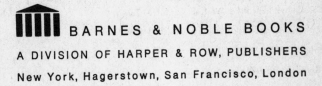
BARNES & NOBLE BOOKS

A DIVISION OF HARPER & ROW, PUBLISHERS

New York, Hagerstown, San Francisco, London

A hardcover edition of this book is published by The Thomas More Press.

It is here reprinted by arrangement.

First BARNES & NOBLE BOOKS edition published 1979

ISBN: 0-06-464029-9

80 81 82 83 10 9 8 7 6 5 4 3 2

CONTENTS

INTRODUCTORY REMARK

The Catholic Position

The publishers have commissioned this book in the expectation that there are people in the world who still care about the "Catholic position." I'm not so sure. There was a time when Catholics looked to the church for answers on everything. Now many of them look to the church for answers to nothing. My own conviction is that both these extremes are based on misunderstanding of the role of the church as teacher. What one might appropriately expect from the church is a limited number of perspectives on the critical issues that are part of the human condition—death, sex, hope, growing old, joy, loneliness, etc. In these one should indeed look to the church for guidance; on other matters, such as the world grain reserve or the law of the sea, one can hardly expect from the church anything more than very vague generalizations. Unfortunately, at the present time Catholic leadership seems far more interested in addressing the second kind of question than it is in providing illumination and perspectives on the first set of issues. (Which may be the reason so few people are listening to them.)

There was a time, of course, when we all believed that there was a Catholic position on almost every conceivable issue from the circumstances under which one could eat meat on Friday to higher education. (I was once denied an appointment as a professor of higher education because of, as one university administrator put it, "the Catholic position on higher education." I sent back word that I would be delighted to learn from this worthy what that position was, because I didn't know it myself.) An expert Catholic was someone able to expound and to defend, if necessary, "the Catholic position" whenever the subject was to be discussed. An outsider thought himself very well informed if he could speak knowingly of "the Catholic position" on at least a select number of issues. From the point of view of the 1970s, the intriguing question is not why we have turned away from "the Catholic position" mentality but why we ever got it in the first place.

The counter-Reformation garrison church, defense of apologetics, the outpouring of papal encyclicals on all conceivable subjects (in addition to apostolic love of letters, papal elocutions, *motu proprios,* etc., etc.) are all perhaps part of the explanation for "the Catholic position" mentality. Such a perspective may have made a good deal of sense when we were a mostly uneducated minority in a mostly hostile nativist environment; it makes much less sense today.

There have always been "Catholic positions," many stands that Catholics take within the framework of what they at least would define as "loyalty to the church." Our counterparts on the European continent have known that; Irish, English, and American Catholics have only begun to realize it in the last fifteen years. For example, we American Catholics always believed that it was the official church teaching that one missed mass on Sunday "under pain of mortal sin." Italian and Hispanic Catholics simply did not and do not take such a precept seriously. More recently, theologians have argued that the Lateran Council which established the Sunday observation had no notion of imposing it in such a way that its violation would be a grave sin. On the other hand, the Swiss theologian Hans Kung has recently argued that habitual failure to participate in Sunday worship is incompatible with the Christian commitment. We have, then, four different "Catholic positions." (1) the old catechism position of Sunday mass attendance under pain of mortal sin; (2) the practice of Latin Catholics which said in effect, "No, we are not so obliged" (a practice recently adopted by American Catholics, approximately half of whom do not believe it is a mortal sin to miss mass on Sunday); (3) the teaching of the theologians who say it was never intended to be an obligation under grave sin; (4) finally Hans Kung bringing the argument full circle by suggesting that failure to attend Sunday mass regularly is incompatible with the Christian life. Which of these positions is *the* Catholic one? The old answer would have been the *official* position; but which one is that? The response of the official church would be, "That position we say is official is official."

Whatever may be said in theory, in practice the official church has not been able to command agreement in many areas with its own stance, and has not taken action against those who disagree. There always has been, in other words, a pluralism of

11

Catholic positions—some official, many tolerated, others marginal. The big change for American Catholics is the realization of this pluralism.

In this volume I shall attempt two things. First of all, in trying to answer the question implied in the topic headings I will stress an underlying Catholic orientation or perspective which I take to be more important than the specific question. Secondly, I will describe the official position, so far as one can be ascertained, the belief and practice of ordinary Catholics, and the speculation of theologians. Sometimes I will express my own opinion, for what it's worth. Readers may decide for themselves what they find acceptable and unacceptable.

ABORTION

Catholic teaching insists that the foetus is a human person and has all the rights of a human person. Hence the termination of the life of a foetus is murder. There is relatively little difference between Protestants and Catholics in America on the question of legalization of abortion. The majority of both religious groups support it under certain circumstances (risk of the life of the mother) and oppose it under other circumstances (a woman simply does not want to have a child). But it is important to note that while Catholics are tolerant of the civil legalization of abortion, they do so as good pluralists, unwilling to impose their own moral beliefs on others. Over 90 percent of American Catholics say that they themselves would not seek an abortion or would not want their spouse to seek one.

Yet the Catholic prohibition against terminating the life of a child is not absolute. Under some circumstances, for example, ectopic pregnancies or a severely diseased uterus, according to Catholic moral theory, operations are licit which de facto will lead to the death of the child. Such termination of pregnancies are justified in light of the moral "principle of double effect": an operation with two results, one good and one bad, with the bad result not flowing from the good one. Of course, once one has conceded the possibility that there are certain kinds of "Catholic abortion," one has acknowledged that the issue is a good deal more complicated than simply a foetus's right to life. There are few if any Catholic theologians who are ready to defend abortion, though some Catholic women activists (not excluding nuns) have campaigned for a woman's right to make her own decision about abortion on the grounds that every woman has a right to make a decision over her own body, as though control over one's body were absolute. (Nobody, as far as I know, would argue that our control over our own bodies is such that we can ingest large amounts of alcohol into the bloodstream and then drive an automobile through a crowd of people on the grounds that we can do whatever we want with our bodies.) However, some Catholics have wondered when human life is present in the foetus. They are completely persuaded that a single fertilized ovum is indeed a human person. The Scholastics in the Middle Ages were not persuaded either, though for reasons that are today perceived as biologically erroneous. The biological and philosophical issues affecting the question of when human life begins in the womb are complicated and perhaps insoluble. Supporters of abortion argue that a human person is present only when a baby is capable of existing outside its mother's womb. (Though some abortion supporters also argue that infanticide is no different from abortion and is a logical consequence of it. They are a small minority, however.)

There are few questions in American society which are more vigorously controverted than the abortion issue. Dialogue between the two sides seems to be extremely difficult. Many Catholics, the present writer included, cannot understand how men and women of good faith and good will do not perceive that a three-months old embryo is indeed human and must be respected as human. It must be said honestly, however, that many abortion supporters are men and women of sincerity, honesty, and good faith. In a civilized society we ought to strive to understand the logic and rationale of their position even if we cannot accept it; and they must strive to understand our position too. But these preliminary dialogues seem quite impossible in the highly emotional atmosphere of the current abortion debate.

Catholics should also realize that while their position is currently described as "unliberal," there was a time, when the anti-abortion laws were written (mostly under Protestant auspices, be it noted), that such protection of the life of the unborn was considered to be a notable and progressive advance for civilization. Abortion and infanticide are the two principal means of population control that the human race has used down through its history. Even as recently as the last part of the nineteenth century, tens of thousands of neonates or foetuses were destroyed every year by exposure, by drowning, by being put out to baby farms. The waters of the Thames and the Seine carried them off by the scores every night of the year. All the churches vigorously opposed abortion and infanticide during the worst of the nineteenth-century epidemic brought on by the population explosion of that time. Catholicism remains true to that liberal and civilized theme; but it does so against the age-old practices of humankind and against the de facto practices of many of its own people in past years. All species practice forms of population control when disease and violent death fail to keep the population within psychologically tolerable limits. The killing of foetuses and babies, appalling as it may seem to contemporary Catholics, has been the response of humankind to population pressures throughout its history, a response which apparently troubled very few consciences. These facts are noted not to defend abortion, not to suggest that Catholics abandon their opposition to it; but simply so that the issue may be seen in the proper historical perspective.

ANNULMENT

Annulment: a form of Catholic "divorce" by which the Church declares two married people free to remarry on the grounds that their first marriage was not in fact a valid sacramental marriage. The grounds for annulment were quite limited until recently—refusal to have children, refusal to grant the sexual act, impotency, a valid prior marriage, explicit intention to exclude a permanent marriage. Most of these had to be proved as existing before the presumed marriage occurred. Recently, however, there has been a notable broadening of the grounds for annulment. The principal new ground is "psychic incompatibility." An annulment is granted when it can be shown that there were sufficient psychological reasons present at the time of the marriage to prevent one or both partners from entering into the kind of contract with one another which would in fact be sacramental. The emotional disturbance involved need not, according to many diocesan marriage tribunals, be completely incapacitating. Indeed, some tribunals now recognize a phenomenon called "relative incapacity," by which is meant that these two particular people, while they may have been able to contract valid sacramental marriages with other persons, could not contract them with one another. The present writer was asked to judge in a certain diocesan tribunal what the difference was between "relative incapacity" and "acute incompatibility." His response was "not very much."

Many Catholics are critical of this route to "Catholic divorce," claiming that it is a sham. However, this criticism seems superficial to the present writer. Broadening the grounds for annulment does not mean that the Church is compromising its teaching on the sacredness of sacramental marriage; it just means that the Church is accepting the psychological advances which reveal to us how difficult it is for people to be mature enough at the time of marriage to make the kind of commitment that in fact mirrors the commitment of Christ and the Church to one another (the theological basis for sacramental indissolubility). Growth into this kind of commitment is seen as a process rather than as a single exchange of words on a given day. How many people, especially young people, are capable of sacramental commitment on their wedding day is problematic. One could argue that some people are prepared and others are not. The bond between a couple may already be "potentially" sacramental before the exchange of vows because of the maturity of their understanding of the commitment to one another. The link between another couple may take considerable growth and development before it matures into a sacrament. It would be well, perhaps, in trying to explain this rather dramatic change in Catholic practice that when annulments are granted the decision in effect is that no sacrament was present, but it is not a decision that there was no marriage; there was at least a civil marriage.

FASTING

We used to do it grimly, protestingly, unhappily, and badly during Lent. We don't do it much any more. The idea was that we fasted to expiate our sins. A lot of people today do not believe in either sin or expiation, but they still fast, often throughout the year, for reasons of physical health or attractiveness. We have, in other words, more dieting and less fasting, which may be a paradox but which is probably a contradiction. Might not Lent and Advent be appropriate times for dieting, times when one takes care of both one's spiritual and physical health by demonstrating resourcefulness, self-discipline, and self-control? Could it be that we have blown a very useful idea on this one?

BAD POPES

Good heavens, does anyone still worry about that? Of course, there have been bad popes—lots of them—just like there have been bad presidents, bad kings, even bad ward committeemen and precinct captains. There may still be some Catholics somewhere in the United States who feel the need to apologize for the fact that the popes and papal electors are human. If the Lord didn't expect there to be some corrupt leadership in His Church, he ought better to have turned it over to archangels.

But the principal problem in the papacy for the last several hundred years has not been corruption (though some of that has been known to occur in the Roman curia and in some dioceses and archdioceses around the world, including the United States) but competency. However one defines the papacy theologically, it is politically and socially a world leadership position of immense importance. The present haphazard means of selecting a pope, while it has lasted a thousand years, is not necessarily the one best suited to produce the kind of leadership a worldwide organization needs in the twentieth century. It could be argued that we could only be sure of relatively competent popes when the base of the papal electorate is notably broadened. On the other hand, we did elect Richard Nixon as President of the United States of America, didn't we? Still, as Winston Churchill remarked, "Democracy is a terrible way to run a government until one considers the alternatives." On balance, therefore, we would probably have much more competent popes if the process of electing them were more democratic. (Presumably, few people agree with the way Cardinal Danilou viewed the election of the pope by the College of Cardinals as of divine origin.) In fact, we would probably have much better bishops if that election base was broadened—perhaps back to the ancient custom of electing bishops through the vote of the clergy and laity of a diocese. Many mayors elected in the United States are incompetent, but by and large a democratically elected mayor is a more impressive and more able leader than a secretly appointed bishop.

TRIDENTINE MASS

The mass said in Latin was according to a form officially approved by the Council of Trent, which in its turn merely refined and clarified a basic structure going back at least to Pope Gregory in the sixth century. There is no real reason why people who want the Tridentine mass shouldn't be permitted to have it, especially since it is clear that the overwhelming majority of Catholics accept enthusiastically the vernacular and reformed mass. Unfortunately, some of the support for the Tridentine mass is based on a doctrinal argument that the post-Vatican II mass is heretical and invalid, an argument which neither Rome nor the majority of Catholics is prepared to admit or even consider. Over the long haul, one can imagine the Tridentine mass will be celebrated on some occasions as a curious museum piece for those who are interested.

Might it not be possible, however, for a priest to exercise the option of saying the *Kyrie* in Greek, the *Sanctus* in Latin and Hebrew (what language do you think *sabaoth* is?), and the *Agnus Dei* in Latin? Such an option would make available to us once again the rich resources of liturgical music from the past and also establish clearly our continuity with an indebtedness to those who went before us. Would it not be good, in other words, to have a mass in four languages—most of it vernacular but with a touch of Greek, Hebrew, and Latin?

INFALLIBILITY

I don't really want to get into this one. I told my good friend Hans Kung that he was making a mistake when he got into it. Clearly Vatican I is on the record as saying that the pope is infallible; but if form criticism is legitimate on scriptures, *a fortiori,* it is legitimate in dealing with conciliar documents. There are doubtless ways that the Vatican I pronouncement could be interpreted today so that it would offend neither our separated brothers nor those Catholics who feel the idea is obscurantist and reactionary. It is most unlikely that a solemn papal exercise in infallibility will ever occur again, and the issue and term should be left alone for the present. There is no reason to choke ourselves on arguments which may have been appropriate to another time and place but not for today.

Is the Church infallible? Sure it is. In what sense is it infallible? I think there are good answers to that question which will be accepted eventually as solid Catholic doctrine but which you can get into a hell of a lot of trouble for stating now. I'm going to leave it to the theologians to work this one out. Let them take their own risks. I don't think it's an issue worth fighting about.

MYSTICISM

The word has many different meanings, but the primary one refers to an intense but transient experience in which the subject feels a direct and immediate union through knowledge of the basic force or forces of the universe. While occasionally some mystical experiences may be negative ("a great cosmic buzz," according to one person who had one such experience), they are normally intensely and often unbearably joyous. They generate feelings of peace, happiness, contentment, security. One feels oneself to be on fire with love and bathed in light—sometimes light which is visibly perceptible. More than one-third of the American population has had such experiences; five percent have had them frequently. Even though the psychoanalytic profession writes such experiences off as a schizophrenic regression to childhood, the empirical evidence indicates that mystics have extremely high scores on measures of psychological well-being and mental health.

Mystical experiences are widespread in all the world religions, and according to some scholars, they may be universal. Some American mystics suggest that those of us who deny that we have such experiences are either repressing them or fooling ourselves. There is a good deal of flakiness currently associated with the active pursuit of such experiences through drugs or other artificial means. In fact, most of the mystics interviewed in our research on the subject report that such experiences are spontaneous, unsought, and often not wanted again (too much joy!).

The Catholic Church presides over the Western world's oldest tradition of mysticism but does so ineptly and uneasily, fearing the self-deception of the false mystic rather than being eager to search the insight of the real mystic. There is currently in some faddist Catholic circles a cult of Eastern mysticism—transcendental meditation and other such fashionable practices—but little willingness to seriously reexamine the rich resources of the great Catholic mystical authors, John of the Cross, Teresa of Avila, Richard Rolle, Juliana of Norwich, etc., etc., etc. Almost certainly there will be a revival in the years ahead of serious spiritual and mystical theology within the Church. Who knows, even spiritual directors might become fashionable again?

FUNDAMENTAL OPTION

Fundamental option: a term developed by some moral theologians to indicate that what matters in a person's life is not so much an individual act as the basic style with which the person lives, the basic orientation of his existence. You will be damned—if you are damned—not because after a sinless life you committed one mortal sin at the very last second of your existence but because insistently and persistently you were narrow, rigid, unloving, cautious, harsh, unforgiving. You will be saved—if you are saved— even if your life was filled with sin and mistakes because you lived a life of generous, open, loving response to the invitation of the heavenly Father as revealed to us by the Lord Jesus.

The fundamental option theme is a very welcome development, because it stresses that salvation does not come from doing certain things but rather from a way of doing everything. That one responds to God's love not by obeying laws but by reshaping one's whole existence. Some shallow interpreters of the funda- mental option theme (the kinds of people, for example, who hear the word in summer school insti- tutes) think it eliminates the need to be concerned about the morality of individual acts. What it does, in fact, is emphasize the obligation beyond obligations, the norm which underpins norms, the law which transcends all laws. One still must be concerned about the morality of individual actions, but one must also realize that a life of blameless morality does not constitute a life of loving response demanded of the followers of Jesus of Nazareth.

CELIBACY

There are, as far as I can see, two solid arguments for celibacy. One is that it frees a person for more intense devotion to the service in the community of God's people. I'm sorry, but I just can't accept the notion that a married Protestant minister, all other things being equal, is as free to serve his people as is the celibate Catholic priest (nor a married doctor, nor a married lawyer, nor any of those other examples that are cited in the arguments against celibacy). Nor is there any evidence from the research done that celibate priests are any more insensitive or incapable of intimacy than are married men of the same age and educational experience.

The second argument for celibacy, the so-called "eschatological" one, used to turn me off, but I think that if one drops the word "eschaton" and talks about "mystery," then the celibate witness is indeed powerful. It means that the people who have made the commitment to lives of generous and intense service in the community of the faithful do so in the name of an invisible but overpowering reality which dominates their lives. The presence of such a reality as reflected in the lives of committed celibates has an impressive and powerful effect on believers and unbelievers alike. It offends, affronts, scandalizes but also astonishes, fascinates, and disconcerts them. Anyone who doesn't think so has never hung around a secular university very long.

Celibacy may very well become optional in the future in the Church; and that will be all to the good, because charismas that are imposed on people are no longer charismas. If celibacy does become optional, it still must be considered one of the impressive treasures of Western Catholicism, one to be protected from destruction by a simple-minded distortion of Freudian psychology, which argues that personal growth and fulfillment can only come to those who share a bed with a member of the opposite sex.

MARRIED PRIESTS

Three-quarters of the American Catholic population could live with the notion of a married clergy, and two-thirds actively support a married clergy—quite likely because they believe the Church would change its teaching on birth control and be more sensitive to the problems of married people if its clergy were married. In fact, however, clergy are as much opposed to the birth control teaching of the Church as are the laity; the problem does not lie in clerical insensitivity but in curial insensitivity. Nevertheless, the laity would certainly not be shocked at having married priests—though they might be shocked at having to pay them and to concede to them the private lives that married men require (and which Protestant ministers and their families rarely receive).

As is clear from the practice of the Eastern Church, there is no incompatibility between the sacrament of matrimony and the sacrament of holy orders. In the Eastern churches religious order priests practice celibacy, parish priests are married. Ironically, in the West the opposite approach might make more sense. The religious orders teach high schools and colleges, which one can do just about as well married or single; it is precisely the parish clergy who ought to be free for the vigorous demands of parochial life in the United States.

It would be naive to expect a change in the practice of celibacy in the immediate future, however sympathetic the laity might be to such a change. The hierarchies of the world at the present time seem almost certainly to be overwhelmingly against it. Part of the problem, in my mind, at any rate, is that once marriage becomes an option it almost becomes an obligation, as both our Eastern and Anglican brothers and sisters have experienced. The unmarried clergyman in a situation of optional celibacy is even more of a threat, and far more likely to be suspected of homosexuality. In the present state of human sexual attitudes, it might be very difficult to preserve celibacy as a valid option. Certainly a change should not occur until some method is found for preserving the celibate option and not de facto eliminate it from Catholic life.

MASTURBATION

The Holy Office recently reasserted that masturbation was indeed a grave sin, but few Catholic moralists today outside of Rome would be prepared to agree, and few confessors would attempt to impose such a doctrine on penitents. The Romans, of course, make a distinction—one very important to remember—between theory and pastoral practice. They will vigorously argue that masturbation (and a lot of other things too) is grievous, heinous sin; but then they quickly add that in pastoral practice, of course, one must be sympathetic to the people who commit such sins and realize that in many, if not most, if not all, cases there are extenuating circumstances. The Roman mentality cannot understand why this seems a cop-out to the northern and western European (and North American) mentality. Our approach would be to say, "Why not just admit that it's not really all that seriously sinful and be done with it? Why not say that in many cases it may not be sinful at all and be done with it?"

There is relatively little evidence that the early Christian writers were concerned about this kind of behavior, and indeed it was with considerable difficulty that St. Alphonsus Liguori managed to persuade the teachers of his era that it was a problem that should be taken seriously by theologians and confessors and forbidden as a grave sin. Part of the problem is that quite apart from religious conviction there is a strong cultural tradition against "wasting the seed" because of the belief that the purpose of the seed is to perpetuate family, clan, or tribe. Particularly in a time of high infant mortality, unlimited fertility was virtually essential to continue the species, or subsegments thereof. Wasting the seed might well seem a serious human problem. The extent to which this cultural imperative affected Catholic moral theological thinking and dictated the principal that only in marriage, indeed in the marriage act, could sexual pleasure be enjoyed ought to be a matter for very careful historical research as the Church tries to reevaluate its sexual ethic and separate the wheat of authentic human wisdom from the chaff of culturally conditioned precepts. It must be said that regrettably little such research is being done in the Church, and apparently the present disposition of the Holy Office is such that little more is likely to be done. It is simply too risky. However, the repetition of prohibitions which no one listens to and which no one probably ever listened to is hardly an effective substitute for attempting to reevaluate so that one can understand more fully the riches of a religious tradition.

PREMARITAL SEX

In discussing this subject one must carefully separate the issue of physical virginity from the issue of sexual love. A strong emphasis on physical virginity is not part of the Catholic Christian heritage; it is a cultural component which attached itself to Catholicism in the ancient world because of the contention that the virginity of a wife was essential to guarantee that one's land and property were truly passed on to one's own seed, to members of one's own tribe. The bride price paid at the time of marriage to the father of the bride was a purchased guarantee of the inviolate hymen of his daughter, a guarantee which was economically important. The cultural norm that has led to an obsession with physical virginity has survived long after it ceased to be economically relevant. The Church has mistakenly permitted its teaching to be infected by this archaic and indeed inhuman attitude.

If Catholics abstain from premarital sex, the reasons have nothing to do with physical virginity and a lot to do with the nature of the Catholic conviction about human love. We believe that human love reflects the single-minded, passionate, total commitment of God to his people, of Christ to his Church; and we are convinced that that central love is only authentically Christian within the context of such commitment. Our chastity is not physical but "mysterious" or eschatological in the sense of revealing, making real, manifesting, demonstrating a higher love which dominates the universe. The ultimate

33

reason why young Catholics should be urged to practice chastity is that followers of Jesus of Nazareth, young people who are committed to reflecting the presence of God in the world, do so by saving their sexual love until it can adequately reflect a single-minded, permanent, passionate commitment. It may be argued that this approach will not convince very many people who do not want to be convinced. So be it; and so much for our failures to explain to young people what Christianity is all about. It might be noted, however, that the argument proposed here is the only one that is truly effective against the attitude, "Well, I've lost my virginity, so now what the hell difference does it make?"

It should also be noted that there is no psychological evidence at all that premarital promiscuity, living together, or any other such arrangements have any effect on the later adjustment of marriage. Indeed, the sexual permissiveness on the college campuses at the present time is frequently just a new form of male exploitation masquerading as ideological liberalism. Chastity may not be a better preparation for marriage, but it is certainly not worse than promiscuity.

Within this framework the question still remains as to whether if marriage is indeed a process (see *Annulment*), need sexual intimacy wait until the formalities of a wedding—especially when a couple is clearly and decisively committed to one another? I'll pass on this one and leave it to moral theologians braver than I to assay an answer. I must say, however, that the moral positions we learned in the seminary, which limited healthy engaged young men and women to quick kisses and gentle hand-holding, seems in retrospect to have been extraordinarily naive and quite possibly psychologically damaging, because it assumed that people could leap from a relationship in which there was no expressed passion to one in which passion was totally expressed within the space of twenty-four hours. Most young people knew better and acted accordingly—with guilty consciences, perhaps, but not feeling they were doing anything "terribly wrong." I do not know where this leaves us on the subject of that favorite teenage sin of yesteryear, "necking and petting," and I defer to the moral theologians and psychologists on the subject. I would simply submit that the Church would be much better advised to use its resources to train its young people in the skills of generosity, patience, and self-sacrifice required for sustained human intimacy instead of harassing them about fondling and passionate kissing. Indeed, one might go so far as to say that the Church would be well advised to seek ways to assure that its young people are capable of maintaining a high level of sexual playfulness after marriage instead of preventing this playfulness before marriage.

Having said all these things, I must add that it is my conviction both as a priest and as a social scientist that religiously, psychologically, and humanly, chastity is far superior to promiscuity, and that in the sexual act there is a built-in strain toward permanence which ought to be taken far more seriously than it is today.*

WEALTH OF THE CHURCH

Given its membership, their resources, and the multitudinous works and services it maintains, the Church probably has far less wealth than it ought to have. One can get wildly exaggerated statements about the wealth of the Church (in the books of Nino LoBello, for example); but these estimates are based on the value of property, and most of the property the Church owns—orphanages, schools, churches, hospitals—are not income-producing and are not easily redeemable on the market for liquid reserves. The Church, indeed, is property poor in the sense that it has vast land holdings which do not produce income but which must be sustained by "deficit financing" (in one way or another out of the Sunday collection). A realistic accounting system (heaven forbid!) of the wealth of the American Church ought to take into account the money that is saved by the rest of society because of the Church's educational and charitable contributions, as well as the "real" (that is, "market") value of romanesque and gothic churches in the open marketplace. The best book on the Church's

* See Andrew M. Greeley, *Sexual Intimacy* and *Love and Play* (Chicago: Thomas More Press, 1973 and 1975 respectively).

36

finances, *Worldly Goods* by James Gollin, suggests that the problem with Church finances is not that the Church has too much money but that given its tasks it has rather too little money. Further, given its commitments it has too many inexperienced, untrained, and inept administrators—the kind of men who think it's wise administration to save string.

American Catholics apparently give far less of their per capita income to the Church than American Jews give to the Jewish community—not because American Catholics are less generous but because American Catholic finance is less imaginative, creative, and vigorous.

The myth of great wealth in the Church delights the hearts of the anti-Catholic nativist bigots and the angry, marginal Catholics. It simply does not correspond to the facts. Would that we did have the money, for example, to fund high-quality research or high-quality staffs in both the local and the national Church.

SAINTS

Some unkind wit remarked recently, "The Church is canonizing more saints than ever before and has fewer saints." In the early times people became saints by acclamation, that is to say, Catholic folks in a given area of the world decided that their bishop or their abbot or their favorite holy person was indeed so holy that he/she was a special friend of God and had to be considered among the ranks of those who had already joined God. Such people were honored, prayed to, imitated, perhaps even worshiped because they were authentic folk heroes. They incarnated and symbolized the dreams, the aspirations, the convictions, the faith of their people. Obviously, such localized and informal canonization process led to all kinds of confusion, abuses, and "quickie" canonizations.

As a part of the centralizing and reforming part of the Counter-Reformation, the elaborate Roman canonization process we now have was established. It means that people can be canonized when religious orders or dioceses are willing to put time, energy, and money into "promoting" a "process." This is great for the members of the religious order and for some people of the diocese involved, but ordinary lay folk, excluded from the process, really couldn't care less. One wonders, for example, how many Philadelphians clapped their hands for joy at the canonization of John Nepomocene Neumann. Sanctity, in other words, has become bureaucratized and dehumanized, which is a shame, because if you have spent any time with the real saints (Dorothy Day or Mother Teresa, to mention two I've encountered), you realize that there are differences of degree, not of kind, between them and the rest of us. Such people ought to be taken seriously at any age of human history not because we can expect to be like them but because they provide impressive illumination on how human beings ought to act toward one another.

RESURRECTION

The central doctrine of Christianity as revealed to us by the Lord Jesus is the depth, the power, the passion, the comprehensiveness of God's love. Within such a vision of God's love it is inconceivable that an all-powerful God could tolerate the passing out of existence of those he loves. Thus, the conviction that human life survives after death—certainly not original with Christianity—becomes one of the core symbols of Catholic Christianity because it is now an indicator of the power, the depth, the intensity of God's amazing love for his creatures. (How come he ever fell in love with us anyway?)

Belief in the resurrection, then, that is to say, belief in the survival of the human personality after death, is an absolutely central and critical component of Catholic Christianity. Those who reject the notion of human survival do so at the risk of separating themselves totally and completely from the Catholic heritage and tradition. We know very little about how this survival occurs or what the life after it is like (except that it will be spectacularly good, for the Lord himself has told us so). The best way a Christian can prepare for death is to develop a great capacity for surprise.

Within this context, the great marvel of Christianity is not the resurrection of a single man—Jesus —but the power of God's passionate love which is so great that all of us will survive death. The resurrection of Jesus is important as a promise and a prelude to the resurrection of us all.

Historically, it is absolutely certain that the apostles experienced Jesus as supremely alive after he had been executed and buried. There is no other explanation for the beginning of Christianity than such an Easter experience of Jesus as still alive. There is no reason to doubt the basic accuracy of the sketchy descriptions of the event that can be found in the early Pauline epistles—though many if not all of the stories in the gospels as we now have them may be theological illustrations rather than historically accurate narratives. What precisely was the *physical* nature of the resurrection of Jesus is very difficult for us to say, because we were not there to observe and take notes. The early Christians were not interested in these things; they were merely interested in the fact that the Lord had died and was now alive. Some theologians argue at great length whether a video tape camera placed in front of the tomb would have recorded the emergence of Jesus. I rather doubt that question has much theological importance, but it has even less religious importance. The critical question is, does Jesus live? The answer of the early Christians, despite the skepticism all around them, was "Yes, he does." And there is no other acceptable answer from any of those who claim to be his followers today. It was no easier then to believe that the Lord is truly risen than it is now, and no easier to believe that his triumph over death is a promise and a prediction of our triumph over death.

EXTRAMARITAL SEX

Before getting into this complex area a number of things must be said about sexual ethics in general, which ought to be kept in mind in reading the replies in this book to specific questions on sexuality:

1. In the basic and fundamental Christian world-view sex is not evil but good, worthy to be the image of God's love for his people and of the Love of Jesus for the Church, the creative, life-giving, life-force dynamic by which humankind continues and expands, the ecstatic hint of the pleasures of union with God, the best anticipation we have of what the joys of eternity will be like, the force within us which breaks down our narrowness and selfishness and drives us into loving union with other humans. Christianity came into existence at a time when the basic world-view—at least of the elite—was profoundly pessimistic and viewed the material world and the human

body as restraints, chains binding the freedom of the human spirit. Sexuality, then, was fundamentally evil, a burden to the human spirit which had to be justified in terms of necessity for continuing the family, the tribe, the clan, the city, the people. This combination of philosophical pessimism and the economic approach to reproduction shaped the matrix in which Christian ethicians thought about sex for most of the Church's history. While it could be argued that the ethicians could have transcended their cultural environment and realized that sexuality is good, such hindsight is irrelevant. One had to break away from the Platonic worldview and from the pagan concern with transmitting family property before an authentically Christian sexual ethic could emerge. One must admit that it took more than 1900 years for this transformation to occur and that only now have we begun to explore the symbols of the Christian religion to find illumination for the ambiguities and dilemmas of human sexuality. However, at least we can be clear now—clearer than most of our predecessors were—that sex is not something evil of which to be ashamed. (It should be noted, incidentally, that the marriage liturgies down through the ages show that there was another tradition within the Church competing with the pessimism and the Manicheism of the theologians which linked sex with love and saw it as a positive, constructive force in the world.)

2. On the other hand, our ancestors were not howling savages and in the traditional wisdom there

42

is much important truth (no matter what the subject). As John Shea has written, Catholic Christians hoard symbols because they are convinced that in the collection of old symbols there can be found many critically important insights which contemporary humans have lost. The art of reconstruction and reevaluation consists in separating the perennial truth within an old symbol from historically determined factors which are no longer relevant. That promiscuity is bad for the individual person and for society, for example, is undoubtedly perennial wisdom; the emphasis on physical virginity to the exclusion of all else is probably not.

3. Even the traditional moral theology contended that the ultimate judge of the morality of the human act or decision was the conscience of the person. One simply cannot provide specific answers to concrete situations from a mathematical or logical application of principle to the situation. Moral decisions, even the old ethnicians taught, must take into account both principles and circumstances. Human intelligence and human decision-making is the essence of morality, and one cannot escape the anguish of making one's own decisions by blindly falling back on principles. Nor can one dismiss principles as totally irrelevant abstractions; they are rather to be thought of as immensely important input variables in moral decision-making calculations. The moral human person, in other words, can escape neither to the chaos of pure situationism, in which anything goes so long as it can be described as "love," or to a neat,

narrow, legalism where every single human decision is clearly and precisely defined by some principle or rule.

4. We humans are extraordinarily skilled at self-deception, and there is no area in which we deceive ourselves more quickly and more effectively than sexuality. Hence, while ultimately we all must make our own individual decisions, we must be especially suspicious of ourselves when we think that our own particular and unique circumstances justify divergence from the accepted wisdom of our own community. We must, in other words, make our own decisions; but we must also strive for reality checks to make sure that our decisions are not self-deceptive and self-destructive—especially when we are dealing with such powerful and suprarational dynamics like sex.

With these four observations kept in mind, one can observe that the current practice of many, probably of most American Catholic confessors and moral advisors is to say that the presumption certainly is always in favor of the traditional ethical norms; but for some persons, under some circumstances, there may be other solutions. Even the Roman moral theology would admit this—but through the back door of "pastoral practice." Thus, from the Roman viewpoint, if a person is in an impossible marriage situation and forms a permanent, loving liaison with another person, this behavior may be "objectively" immoral; but the person may well be in "subjective" good faith in his/her decision, and the confessor or advisor ought to be kind and sympathetic in dealing with such a person. Whether one then follows the American system of saying that sometimes persons and circumstances are exceptional or the Roman system of dealing sympathetically with those who are in difficult situations and have strong subjective good faith, the practical conclusion is the same: no general principle is an absolute and inflexible guide for human ethical behavior.

"THE THIRD WAY"

A number of years ago young priests and religious began to use this term to describe intense human intimacy that was not marital but went beyond the traditional practices of ecclesiastical celibacy. There was a good deal of empty and unrealistic psychological cant in the discussion of "the third way," and many of its practitioners are more or less happily married to one another. But the immaturity of "the third way" conversation should not obscure the fact that the old Catholic approach to intimacy left something to be desired both humanly and historically.

It is impossible to divide all human relationships into those between married persons, which are passionately intense, and all others, which are void of passion and eroticism. Any strong human friendship inevitably has an erotic component because we humans are erotic in every cell of our bodies. The Catholic tradition knows many varieties of intense friendships which surely were erotic in some sense but not genital. The early, informal Christian communities of both men and women together during the persecution years, the *agape* (co-ed) monasteries of Asia and then of Ireland (where they lasted well into the sixth century), the ideal and practice of romantic love in the Middle Ages (which were at least partially Christian), the close friendships between men and women saints, the friendships that priests, religious, and even well known archbishops and cardinals have in the present time (virtually all of which seem to be healthy and constructive relationships) are all examples of intimate, non-genital relationships. Admittedly the possibility of such relationships was denied by several generations of novice masters and mistresses and spiritual directors. In this respect they made common cause on the one hand with the locker room sexuality which views everything as lewd and Freudian determinism which views everything short of total genitality as unhealthy and frustrating on the other hand. There is, in other words, a fantastic pluralism of human intimacies which are both moral and growth-producing regardless of rigid categories of gender, marital status, or state in life. Such relationships are surely dangerous and must be approached cautiously. They are easily misunderstood, and the risks of self-deception and exploitation are large. Certainly they are not for the immature. However, all of these comments could be made about marital intimacy too. But they are to be made more strongly about nonmarital, nongenital intimacy. It does not follow that such intimacy should be avoided completely; rather, it should be dealt with cautiously, discreetly, patiently, quietly. Almost as a rule of thumb, one might say that a person who vigorously and enthusiastically describes his/her "special" relationship on virtually every occasion is headed for trouble.

Many people who tentatively explore such relationships ask questions about what is permitted them. ("May we kiss?" "May we be naked with each other?") These are virtually unanswerable. Surely, no hard and fast principles can be applied to such intimacies save for the fact that only those who are strong and firm in their main life commitments should even consider experimenting with them. We simply do not have available yet the kind of folk wisdom which makes advice possible beyond individual cases. It is, however, more than just a cliche to say that such people should not be afraid to take risks, because everything in life is risky, but they should be cautious in their risks, because uncalculated risks can be destructive of human happiness.

DIVINITY OF JESUS

The traditional Catholic conviction that Jesus was a man like us and yet that God was present in him in a special and unique way in which he was present in no other human being has been expressed in the formularies of the early councils through the terminology of one person (Divine) and two natures (Human and Divine). The principal point in the mystery of Jesus as God and man is that in Jesus God's love is most fully and adequately revealed to us. Many people don't seem to see this point and get hung up on the theological explanations of how God is present in Jesus instead of understanding the why of God's presence in Jesus. When someone is "having trouble with the faith" and says that he/she doesn't believe in the divinity of Jesus, what they are normally rejecting is the monophysite or docetist heresies which deny the humanity of Jesus—heresies which have been very strong throughout Christianity and still influence the way many Catholics persist in thinking about Jesus. At one time in history, the Church's major efforts were expended in defending the humanity of Jesus. In these days of *Godspell, Superstar,* etc., it would appear that God's special presence in Jesus is what is under attack. Yet many conservative Catholics are still uneasy at the suggestion that Jesus was man. They seem to feel that his divinity can only be protected by denying his humanity. The authentic Catholic position maintains a balance, a tension, between the two truths. Theologians are currently wrestling with formulas which are more adequate to express these truths than the ones we have from the Councils of Ephesus and Chalcedon—especially since "person" and "nature" hardly mean today what they did in the past.

ENCYCLICALS

Encyclical letters sent by the pope to all the bishops of the world were a major means of transmitting papal teaching to the faithful of the world. Some of them are doctrinal, such as the encyclical *Humani Generis,* condemning the "new theology"; others are moral, such as the unsuccessful encyclical *Humanae Vitae,* forbidding birth control in 1968; still others were social, such as the classic *Rerum Novarum* and *Quadragesimo Anno.* The height of the social encyclical tradition was the famous *Pacem in Terris* of Pope John XXIII, a document which had worldwide influence. These social encyclicals were a serious and very successful attempt to articulate the Catholic social tradition. Pope Paul's contribution to the social encyclical, *Popolorum Progressio,* was much less successful (as were most of his other encyclicals) largely because the staff that prepared the document for him departed in many fundamental ways from the Catholic social heritage and turned to a warmed-over version of anti-American Marxism.

INQUISITION AND GALILEO

Oh, come on, fellas, you've got to be kidding! Nobody expects anyone to defend the Inquisition and the Galileo case any more, do they? The Inquisition was a disastrous mistake, as is its lineal descendant the Congregation of the Holy Office (and nobody, but nobody, calls it by its new name, Congregation of the Faith). The basic assumption on which the Inquisition—even its most unobjectionable form—was based was that faith is something that must be tenaciously defended and protected. The early Christians quite properly thought that faith is something that ought to be joyously proclaimed. They were content to leave its protection to God. The sooner the Holy Office and all its pomps and works is abolished, the better off the church will be. Other more discreet and more hopeful ways can be found to define the outer perimeters of orthodoxy. There is no point trying to apologize for the Galileo case. We were just wrong, that's all.

ITALIAN POPES

The last non-Italian pope was Adrian VI back in the early 1600s. It has been remarked by a number of observers that it is indeed curious that the Holy Spirit, who is supposed to preside over papal elections, does not seem to think that people of other national backgrounds are qualified to run the Church. Even Italian Catholics will tell you today that they only hope for reform of the Italian Church when a pontiff is elected who is not Italian. There is some theological argument about the nature of the papacy. Is the pope primarily the Bishop of Rome, or is he primarily head of the Universal Church? If he is the latter, then there is surely no reason why non-Italians should not be elected. If he is the Bishop of Rome, as some progressive theologians have suggested, then perhaps he ought to be Italian; but then the whole structure of world governance needs to be abolished. A number of progressive theologians, including the editors of *Concilium,* in their special issue on papal elections, have done a profound disservice to the Church by arguing that the pope is mostly Bishop of Rome and should continue to be Italian. If they are right in theory (which seems problematic in a time when all multinational leadership transcends local boundaries—like the Archbishop of Canterbury, for example, or the General Secretary of the World Council of Churches. In practice these theologians merely aid and abet the efforts of the Roman curia to keep its stranglehold on Catholic life. De facto, the pope has become a world figure; it is inconceivable that he will ever stop being one. To insist on theological grounds, either conservative or liberal, that men of only one nationality should occupy that position seems mindless.

RELIGIOUS LIFE

Since the very beginning of the Church there have been men and women who have chosen to dedicate themselves in a special way to the work of the Church or to lives of prayer and meditation. This choice became institutionalized fairly early in the Church's history in the religious orders or the religious life. Now such a life is defined by canon law as existing when people take public vows of poverty, chastity, and obedience. The religious life has had its ups and downs. The communal Monasticism of Benedict replaced in great part the hermit life of the desert monks (and of the early Irish monasteries, too, for that matter). The wandering friars of the Middle Ages (Benedictines, Franciscans, Dominicans, principally) supplemented the work of the relatively immobile monks; the clerks regular at the time of the Reformation (Jesuits, for example) and the congregations of the later years (Vincentians, for example) all represent adjustments of the theme of the religious life to the changing world environment. At present the religious life seems to be in a great deal of trouble in the United States. Perhaps the insights of the founding geniuses of the communities all too quickly became rigidified and institutionalized by inflexible, canonical regulations. The attempts to "modernize" the religious orders in the wake of the Vatican Council were largely unsuccessful apparently because the changes were based on very shallow theology and social science. Many of those who won the battles of reforming their chapters, revamping their communities, then left because they had destroyed the strong authority structure of the community, which they needed both to lean on and to hate. The massive exodus of men and women from the religious orders and the very low levels of new vocations raise the possibility at least that most of the present religious orders will disappear. Surely the frantic leaping from fad to fad which constitutes many contemporary religious suggests an attitude approaching panic. However, it seems very doubtful that a form of service which has responded to human needs and aspirations for almost two millennia will disappear overnight. What new forms of religious life may emerge is still unclear, though they are likely to include both men and women and both married and single people. (Canon law will catch up eventually to the idea of married religious.)

As to the present religious orders, it does not seem to have occurred to any of their leadership that before folding up their tents and stealing off into the hills (or, alternatively, the picketlines) they might do some high quality research on how young people view the religious life and what modifications might attract them to vocations.

BERNARD LONERGAN

Bernard Lonergan is perhaps the most influential Catholic theologian of the era. A Canadian of Irish ancestry, Lonergan taught for many years in Rome and now has his base in the Jesuit community in Toronto, Canada. Lonergan is a "transcendental Thomist," that is to say, a disciple of St. Thomas in the tradition of Ambrose Marechal (a theologian in the early years of this century) rather than the traditional and very rigid Thomism that dominated Catholic theology in the years before the council. In this respect Lonergan is related to the German Karl Rahner and the French theologians who were condemned by Rome in the 50s. Not altogether facetiously it has been said that Lonergan escaped the notice of the Roman authorities and influenced vast numbers of students and young scholars at the Gregorian University in Rome because the folks in the curia simply could not understand what he was talking about. Indeed, he does not make easy reading, but his thought is monumentally important. Among the most useful interpretations are *The Achievement of Bernard Lonergan* by David Tracy (a book which led Father Lonergan to remark that some day he would write a book called *The Achievement of David Tracy*) and *Religion and Self-Fulfillment* by John Haught, a brilliant college textbook based on Lonergan's perspective and fully authenticated by the maestro himself.

LIBERATION THEOLOGY

A bizarre idea that the Church, having utterly fouled up in Latin America by being on the side of right-wing extremists, can now redeem itself by going over to left-wing extremists just at the time when a younger generation of philosophers has begun to emerge in France who strongly question whether Marxism is all that radical. The Church in Latin America, with the unerring instinct to climb aboard a sinking ship, has opted for authoritarian Marxist societies under the guise of liberation. Some American Catholic thinkers, apparently constitutionally incapable of reflecting on the experience of their own people, have become enthusiastic supporters of liberation theology. Nowhere among the Latin American, the European, or the North American liberation theologians is there the slightest recognition of the fact that detailed political, social, economic analysis is required to understand social problems and begin to talk intelligently about their solutions. The problems of the poor countries, you see, have all been caused by the rich countries—particularly by the United States. Liberation insists essentially of blaming the United States and demanding that it expiate its sins. The only ones who are really liberated by liberation theology are the oppressive Third World governments who are liberated from taking responsibility for their own political and economic problems, since the gringo devil makes such a marvelous scapegoat.

CHARISMATIC RENEWAL

An enthusiastic movement borrowed by some of the high churches (most notably Roman Catholic and Anglican) from fundamentalist Protestants. The movement is marked by spontaneous prayer, faith-healing, and speaking with tongues. Some charismatics argue that it is actually the Holy Spirit who speaks in the glossolalia, while others, more responsible, suggest—with considerable social science evidence to support them—that the glossolalia is enthusiastic nonverbal speech. One might call it happy and harmless babbling, perhaps even prayerful happy and harmless babbling. Because of its enthusiastic nature, the charismatic movement is prone to anti-intellectualism, synthesism, rigidity, sectarian internal conflict, and authoritarianism. None of these traits need be irresistible. The research of Father Joseph Fichter has raised the possibility that for many Catholics the step into the charismatic movement is a step on the way out of the Church to an even more enthusiastic fundamentalist Protestantism. On the other hand, the charismatic renewal is clearly the most vital and active movement in American Catholicism today, and responds to the religious needs and aspirations of many, many Catholics. Some groups are quite sophisticated theologically and quite restrained psychologically and emotionally while others are fanatics of the sort that the late Monsignor Ronald Knox described in his famous book, *Enthusiasm* (which ought to be read by every Catholic charismatic just to make sure that he/she and his/her group are not going the route to enthusiastic self-destruction). The Catholic hierarchy in the United States is cautiously supportive of the charismatic renewal because of the apparent piety of so many of its members and because it seems relatively harmless. The present writer, who believes the Holy Spirit can speak in English if he wants to, wishes the hierarchy would be more cautious and discriminating, more aware of the history of enthusiastic movements and more conscious of the human and institutional damage that can be done by unrestrained and unguarded enthusiasm.

DEMONIC POSSESSION AND EXORCISM

It is self-evident that there is evil in the world—not only physical evil but human evil, indeed evil which transcends the evil of the individual human actors involved. (Think of the Vietnam war launched by well-meaning and sincere men, the concentration camp holocaust launched by petty and bland men, the destructiveness in American society that came from the Kennedy and King assassinations accomplished by crazy men.) St. Paul's point that our wrestling is with principalities and powers is empirically demonstrated every day in newspapers. We do not fully understand why this conflict between good and evil should rage in the cosmos, in human society, and in our own individual personalities; but that the conflict is there is undeniable. It is not clear at the present time whether we need to fall back on the concept of personalized evil to deal adequately with the presence of evil in the world. It is even less certain that evil can in fact take possession of individual personalities. The Church, quite properly, traditionally has been skeptical in such cases of possession, though it has not hesitated to permit virtuous and well-trained priests to pray over people who are apparently possessed. Most of the American cases of possession which have received attention in recent years, including the one about which the famous movie was made, are quite evidently cases of acute mental illness that have been aggravated by the mumbo jumbo of the exorcism ceremony. Accounts of possession and exorcism are great for terrifying entertainment. At the present writing, TV seems to have caught up with the possession craze. I wish that the Church and churchmen were less willing to cooperate in such endeavors and more ready to vigorously insist that there are far more important evils in the world than titillating cases of alleged diabolic possession.

HOMOSEXUALITY

We understand very little about the psychological and possibly physiological dynamics of homosexuality. At present, serious psychological thinking conceptualizes homosexuality as a case of arrested psychosexual development—though this is obviously little more than a description. The American Psychiatric Association has voted (by no means unanimously) to consider homosexuality not to be a mental illness. However, progress in understanding human behavior is not made by taking votes. Whether it is an illness or not, homosexuality is clearly a dramatic deviation from ordinary human sexual behavior (though there may be strong strains of bisexuality in many people). Traditional Catholic sexual morality, recently reiterated by the Holy Office, considers homosexual acts to be seriously sinful; but the Holy Office quite explicitly evokes the distinction between doctrine and practice and urges pastoral sympathy in dealing with the homosexual. One Holy Office expert went so far as to admit that he would have no trouble counseling a homosexual to seek a permanent liaison because it was the lesser of two evils when compared to casual relationships. Moral practice among many American priests for some time has taken for granted that most homosexuals are "incurable"; that is to say, it is impossible to convert them into heterosexuals. Accordingly, they have been sympathetic and compassionate in dealing with such individuals. The gay liberation movement within the Church, however, would insist on more; it demands full support for equal rights for homosexuals and the acknowledgment that homosexuality is simply an alternative form of sexual activity, no better and no worse than heterosexuality. There is an instinctual reluctance on the part of many Catholics to make that admission. One can, of course, support equal rights for homosexuals and oppose cruelty to them and discrimination against them without agreeing with such a statement. Some Catholic authorities have opposed local ordinances guaranteeing the rights of homosexuals on the grounds that they wish to retain the option of not hiring homosexuals to teach in their schools for fear that such people will attempt to solicit sexual partners from among the students. The gay rights leadership responds that heterosexuals have also been known to solicit sexual partners from among students and that there is no justification for an a priori prejudice against a particular homosexual teacher. To this the response is often made that heterosexuals are much more likely to form permanent liaisons than homosexuals; hence homosexuals will be on the average more likely to seek temporary partners from among their students. Even if such a comment is true, it might still be responded that an individual homosexual whose record in dealing with students is blameless is a victim of prejudice in the strict sense of the word if he is excluded from a job simply on the basis of averages.

It certainly does seem to be the case that the homosexual life is a distinctly unhappy one. There is not the built-in strain toward permanence as in relationships between men and women—though it remains to be seen whether this is a physiological and psychological phenomenon or merely the result of the culture in which a hostile "straight" society compels "gays" to live. Some Catholics who find self-justification in pursuing the most recent fads are currently on the gay liberation bandwagon. Homosexuals should realize that such folk make very poor long-term allies.

INTERCOMMUNION

Catholic theory currently forbids the sharing of Holy Communion with Christians of other denominations on the grounds that in some cases their Eucharist is not valid and in all cases the integrity and authenticity of the Catholic faith is being compromised by receiving communion with heretics or schismatics. (Though we don't quite use those words any more.) The Lord Jesus, in other words, who loved publicans and sinners, would not want to go to men and women of good faith and good will who don't happen to be Roman Catholics. You can get into a lot of trouble in some parishes in some dioceses for giving communion to a non-Catholic; on the other hand, despite the condemnation from Rome and the national hierarchy, intercommunion is frequent and almost epidemic. Ecclesiastical authority has not been able to prevent it and probably will not be able to do so.

ECUMENISM

Originally the word meant the search for unity among the Christian churches. In recent times it has been broadened to include conversation to find common ground between Christians and non-Christians, people of the book, like the Jews and the Moslems, members of other religions such as Hindus, Buddhists, and even nonbelievers and atheists. Ecumenical conversations and the search for, if not unity then common ground, have been very successful. Scholars, ministers, and ecumenical bureaucrats have worked out many statements of agreement; but there seem to be three major barriers to ecumenism: (1) the profound suspicion of ecumenism in the Roman curia, which has effectively sabotaged most practical ecumenical steps of the council; (2) grass roots resistance to the watering down of doctrinal purity (the right wing of the Missouri Synod of the Lutheran church will not even dialogue with other Lutherans); (3) fundamental differences of style and worldview which still exist between Protestants and Catholics. However much common statements may be developed on original sin, for example, the Protestant style and worldview still takes a much more pessimistic view of human nature (and human fun, like gambling, dancing, drinking, card-playing, and sex) than does the traditional Catholic worldview. These differences —clearly evident to social researchers—have been largely ignored by theologians. However, David Tracy, in his forthcoming book *The Analogical*

Imagination, begins a serious discussion of this problem. It is very likely that the church unity toward which we are all working (save for the curial bureaucrats and their counterparts in some of the right-wing denominations) will be a denominational unity and not the unity of a superchurch.

EVOLUTION

Cut it out, you really don't expect me to talk about this, do you? All right. For the record, Catholic teaching (in the encyclical *Humani Generis*) is that it does not appear to be possible to reconcile Polygenism (the human race appearing spontaneously from many different prehuman couples) with monagenism. However, more recent theories of original sin do not seem to encounter this difficulty. Beyond that issue, virtually all Catholic opposition to evolution has vanished—mostly because of the insight that if God works out his designs slowly and gradually instead of abruptly, his style is even more impressive. At what stage of the game "homo" became present (that is to say, from the theological viewpoint a human soul was present) is very hard to estimate; it may be the wrong question to ask. The archeological research being done in East Africa, however, suggests that humans rather like us have existed for hundreds of thousands—perhaps millions—of years, and that the other humanlike creatures that have been discovered represent offshoots or parallel developments or deviant processes. It is a fascinating archaeological, biological, and philosophical question to which the answers are obscure and about which, in the case of the philosophers, very little serious thinking is currently being done. As far as I know, nobody is worried about it theologically anymore. God makes the world work the way he wants it to work and not the way professors at Roman seminaries think he ought to have made it work.

COMMUNION IN THE HANDS

The American hierarchy, after considerable debate, much hand-wringing, and dire warnings from Cardinal Carberry, has finally managed to muster support for a resolution that makes it possible for the laity to receive communion in the hands, this after several score other hierarchies, including the Irish, made the same monumental change. Prolonged and acrimonious debate on critical and major issues like this is just what the Church needs more of. On the other hand, there is no reason why you have to take it in your hands.

CATHOLIC-JEWISH RELATIONSHIPS

In the United States Catholic-Jewish relationships are probably better now than they have been at any time in history and also probably better than they are anywhere else in the world. Nonetheless, there is substantial tension remaining between the two groups, tension which occasionally can become nasty in complex urban environments. Some Jews and some Catholics engaged in "ecumenical" dialogue with Jews think that it is only appropriate for Catholics to approach Jews in a posture of humility and guilt for the persecutions of the past—a rather unecumenical approach to dialogue, by the way. Indeed, according to such authorities, the existence of anti-Catholic feeling among certain Jews simply ought not to be discussed because of "twenty-three centuries" of Catholic persecution of Jews (as Father Edward Flannery has remarked. How a church that has only existed for 1900 years at the most can indulge in 23 centuries of persecution escapes lesser personages than Father Flannery), and whether in a pluralistic environment like the United States a one-sided dialogue can ever be successful seems problematic. However, as one who once spoke out at the insistence of the American Jewish Committee on the presence of some anti-Catholic feeling among some Jews, I serve due notice on everyone that it's a very dangerous subject. You can lose all kinds of grants from foundations and government agencies if you dare to say anything on the subject. Nor will you get any support from Catholic liberals either—no matter how much they may bitch off the record about the Jewish "domination" of American cultural life. Jews, incidentally, don't dominate American cultural life, but they have strong influence in it—not through any conspiracy but through hard work and talent. Still, I know of one Jewish television reporter who got in a lot of trouble for suggesting there was a Jewish lobby on the Israel question in Washington. American Catholics, incidentally overwhelmingly support the state of Israel, though some Jews reject the evidence of the survey data on this subject, saying that Catholics can't support Israel because the pope has not officially recognized the existence of Israel. They give the pope far more power over the political thinking of Catholics than he has—perhaps even than he would like to have. One better not suggest to such people that such judgments about American Catholics are a sign of "prejudgment" or "prejudice."

ANTI-CATHOLICISM

Senator Daniel P. Moynihan recently suggested that anti-Catholic nativism is the most persistent of all American bigotry and will be the last one to be eradicated. It will be the last one to go precisely because American Catholics, particularly intellectual leaders, are not only not willing to fight it but are willing to accept the judgments about their own inferiority made by the non-Catholic intellectual elites. Anti-Catholicism as a political issue, Senator Moynihan argues, may well have disappeared in American society within the 1960 presidential election; it has not disappeared as a cultural issue; indeed, the social and intellectual elites of our country are permeated by a subtle but vicious anti-Catholic bigotry. Those of us who earn our livings and represent the Church in this area experience it almost every day. The quintessential expression of it came to me from a social science colleague who said to me in all fair-minded seriousness, "Women, Jews, and blacks have been underrepresented in the great universities because of prejudice; Catholics are underrepresented because their faith makes them intellectually inferior." But most American Catholics are not suffering any particular financial loss because of anti-Catholic discrimination in the elites and hence are not really concerned to fight it. However, a younger generation of Catholic scholars and writers (mostly in their thirties) are getting more and more fed up with it and are beginning to fight back. For further details and documentation, see my *Ugly Little Secret: The Persistence of Anti-Catholic Nativism* (Kansas City: Sheed Andrew McMeel, 1977).

ORAL SEX

Traditional Catholic morality disapproved of oral sex (and other kinds of fun and games) between a man and wife not on the grounds that these actions were "perverse" but that they would lead to the "wasting of the seed" or were in fact a form of "birth control." Thus the traditional Catholic morality had no objection to oral sex (or other varieties, too, for that matter) so long as the marriage act was finally "completed" in the proper way. Little attention was paid to the acrobatic antics that might be involved in completing such behavior "in the proper way." But now that the overwhelming majority of Catholics have rejected the Church's teaching on birth control they apparently see less reason for worrying about how oral sexual play achieves full satisfaction. There is every evidence that a substantial number of American Catholics, especially younger ones, engage in oral sexual behavior with no guilt feelings and no compulsion to report it to their confessors. On the other hand, it must be insisted, some sex manuals to the contrary, that there is no obligation to engage in oral sex, that one is not a deviant if this particular variety of fun and games does not happen to be of particular interest. There is a middle course that must be steered on the question of sexual technique; it is certainly not unimportant, in keeping the love between a man and a woman vital and growing. All things being equal, the better one's technique the better one's love life will be. On the other hand, if sheer technique could guarantee happy marriages and sexual fulfillment, it would certainly have done so many years ago, given the abundance of manuals providing information, illustrations, and advice which make the Kama Sutra seem unimaginative by comparison. Patience, persistence, kindness, tenderness, compassion, sensitivity, willingness to take risks, to say "I'm sorry," to begin again, to listen, to learn, to grow, to probe gently but firmly the mystery of the other's personhood—all of these are far more important than technique. But that does not make technique unimportant.

SEXUAL DYSFUNCTION CLINICS

These institutions have grown up in many places around the country recently. They engage in "behavior modification" therapy for the most part. The promise of such therapy is that if one can change certain behavior patterns in a couple's lovemaking, then one can, if not eliminate, at least minimize the effect of underlying personality variables that may be at work. In many cases such clinics deal directly (very directly indeed) with problems of frigidity, impotence, and, especially, shame. Only preliminary data are available on how effective such therapy is, though the preliminary data, it must be admitted, is promising. While some of the techniques used in some of the centers may be objectionable, there can be no reasonable Catholic objection to the basic idea of trying to help a man and woman overcome incapacitating problems in their sexual life together. One of the best sexual dysfunction clinics, in fact, is at the Loyola University Medical School in Chicago. On the other hand, the advice *caveat emptor* (let the buyer beware) applies with special vigor to those hunting for such clinics.

PORNOGRAPHY

Both the United States Supreme Court and traditional Catholic ethical theory would define pornography as erotic literature and art which appeals primarily to the prurient interests of those who consume it. Pornographic materials have been available to humankind as far back as we can find traces of human behavior. They are more available in contemporary America (because of Supreme Court decisions) than in previous times in American culture, but probably less available still than in earlier interludes of human existence. The problem of pornography is complicated by the fact that the distinction between the pornographic and the merely erotic is often difficult to make. What will excite the prurient interest of one person may seem to be authentic art (thought perhaps of only meager value) to another. As usual, the Supreme Court has made a godawful mess of the pornography issue. On the other hand, it is clear that *Lady Chatterly's Lover* is not prurient and has considerable artistic merit despite the fact that it was banned for many years, while *Hustler* is virtually devoid of artistic merit. It does not seem possible to make a case against pornography on the grounds that it excites the prurient imagination of adolescents. It is the nature of the adolescent of the species that he has a prurient imagination, and virtually anything excites it. There is no evidence at all—despite confident proclamations to the contrary by some church leaders and even some judges—that pornographic literature

71

leads to sexual crimes and sins. Nonetheless, a case can be made against it on the grounds that it is usually degrading, exploitive trash. Attempts to bar access by young people to all pornographic materials, while certainly legitimate, are not likely to be effective. If there is dirt to be found in anything, kids will find it. The presence of "soft core" or "medium core" porn like *Playboy* and *Penthouse* on the newsstands (and *Playgirl* too) merely mean that it's cheaper and easier for young people to indulge their curiosity about the bodies of the opposite sex. One need not approve of, much less praise, such literature if one says that there is no evidence that it does anyone any great deal of harm. All the available research, as well as most of what we know in psychological theory, suggests the attitudes of young people toward sex are shaped by their parents' attitudes toward it and by the sexual ambiance of the relationship between their mothers and fathers. Parents who engage in antipornography crusades are certainly free to do so, as are parents who resolutely and diligently search the dresser drawers of their children to confiscate the latest copy of *Playboy* or *Penthouse*. These parents should realize that it is far more important that the young people perceive, however implicitly or indirectly, that between the parents there is a healthy, generous, unexploitive sexual tenderness. Indeed, there is every reason to believe that far more harm is done to adolescents by the conviction that their parents do not have sex with one another (whether it is because they do not in fact have sex or because the

72

sexual bond between them is so muted as to be invisible) than by their reading pornographic magazines.

BIRTH CONTROL

The official Catholic position as expressed by the encyclical letter *Humanae Vitae* is that all forms of artificial birth control (all forms other than the rhythm method or total abstinence, in other words) are immoral. The basic argument of the encyclical is that this is the teaching of Christ (though obviously we have no record in the scriptures of any such teaching); such is the traditional teaching of the Church (though in the nineteenth century the Church was silent in the face of massive birth control in France through withdrawal), and because of the natural law of prohibition of artificial birth control (though only Catholic theologians seemed to have managed to find such natural law prohibition). The overwhelming majority of Catholics all over the world seem to have rejected this encyclical (85 percent in the United States, 75 percent in England, 65 percent in Ireland, etc., etc.). It is not the purpose of the present book to discuss the controversy over the encyclical. However, it must be noted that birth control has become part of the family life and of the sexual practices of virtually all contemporary Catholics. Their clergy do not vigorously oppose this (indeed four-fifths of the priests will give absolution to those who are practicing birth control) and their hierarchy, despite high-sounding statements on the subject, rarely if ever does anything to enforce them. It must be said candidly that Church leaders do not seem able to understand what demographers have told them about human fertility. You could make a very convincing argument for unlimited fertility when such high levels of reproduction were required to sustain the human race in existence. Well into the nineteenth century, in most of the peasant places in Europe, the average fertile woman would have to have 6.48 children simply to assure that she would produce one fertile daughter who would continue human reproduction into the next generation; 6.48 children could mean 10 or even 12 pregnancies. A dozen pregnancies, in other words, would normally produce only 2 children who would live to begin their own reproductive cycles. But the advances made in public health, infant mortality, and agricultural production are such that among white people in America 6.48 live births will mean 6.48 teenagers; 12 pregnancies can easily mean 12 adults, a six-fold increase in human population. To say that such a dramatic change does not affect natural law norms on human reproduction does not seem very reasonable.

CONTRACEPTIVE MENTALITY

Some Catholic theologians and teachers who oppose birth control have argued that the legitimation of birth control leads to a "contraceptive mentality," that is, to an attitude and style of life in which personal selfishness permits no time for childbearing and child rearing. The basis of this argument seems to be the notion that unless you force men and women to have children under pain of mortal sin they will not do so. One cannot, in other words, permit people to make their own decisions because if one does, then people won't do the right thing. It's undoubtedly the case that there has appeared in the United States in recent years an expression of the contraceptive mentality among the young people who grew up during the 1960s. Having children has gone out of fashion; one almost has to explain why one has brought a child into the world in certain elite groups. The reasons for this antichild mentality are many: (1) a substantial proportion of the young people in question grew up during the time of the "baby boom." "Baby boom" generations usually produce fewer children than "baby bust" generations, if only because the booms are more aware of the complexities of life in a large family.

(2) The ideology of the woman's movement has said falsely that a woman cannot have a career and be a mother at the same time.

(3) Children are terribly expensive to rear and educate, and young people are appalled at the tre-

mendous "obligation" they take on when they have a child.

(4) Psychologically more sophisticated than any of their predecessors (but still not really sophisticated), many of the young people with the contraceptive mentality feel that the difficulties in assuming psychological responsibility for another human being are such as to be completely beyond their skills. ("Our parents fouled up on us," they will say. "Why should we foul up another generation?")

(5) Finally, many such people are simply afraid of having children, afraid of the responsibility, afraid of the challenge, afraid of the burden, afraid of the expense, afraid of the risks, afraid of the mistakes they may make—just plain afraid. Oddly enough, once they have children they seem to delight in their offspring and, characteristically, act as though they invented parenthood. Recently there are signs that men and women approaching thirty who did not plan to have children are having them, apparently deciding to take the big risk.

The Church obviously has been unable to speak effectively to such young people and their fears—in part because the Church has lost all credibility in areas of sexuality and reproduction by its birth control decision and in part because ecclesiastical authorities would sooner denounce the contraceptive mentality than try to sympathize with and understand the young people who are caught in it. Also Church leaders still cannot adjust to the fact that they are no longer able to "make" people do what they (the Church leaders) feel they should do.

NUDITY (IN ART)

Despite the persistent efforts of generations of puritans and prudes the human body, particularly when it is not grossly overweight, is erotically attractive. It has been designed to be erotically attractive in order to continue the human race and in order to open us up to generosity and unselfishness. The body is quite attractive when clothed, too, and it is perhaps most attractive of all when it is partially clothed, in various stages of dress and undress. The puritans have not been able to prevent artists and sculptors from creating images of the human body in which the body looks attractive and erotic. Nor have they been able to prevent writers from describing in their stories the eroticism which is an integral part of human existence. Not all good art is nude, not all nude art is good; but fig leaves and such-like in the Vatican museum and the Sistine Chapel, as well as everywhere else in the world where such grotesque concessions to puritanism are made, are nothing more than a laughable attempt to pretend that we are not born with genitalia or that these genitalia are not an important part of our existence.

NUDITY (IN DRESS)

One must distinguish carefully between shame and modesty, even though in the personalities of most of us these two reactions are intertwined continuously. Shame is the erroneous obsession which leads us to believe that our bodies and our bodily functions are ugly, dirty, unworthy, and worthless. Modesty is a constructive and healthy human virtue which leads us to reserve that which is most intimate about us for those with whom we are most intimate. Shame is a vice which Catholic Christians should resist; modesty is a virtue which they should develop in themselves and attempt to pass on to their children.

Diversity of circumstance, culture, persons, and situations are such that it is practically impossible to lay down strict and universal judgments about modesty. What is "appropriate garb" depends greatly on the circumstances. The swimming garb which women wore for the first several decades of this century was clearly inappropriate because it made swimming difficult. Some of the more recent swimwear fashions—whatever their other merits may be—apparently makes swimming equally difficult, though for opposite reasons. A bikini may be modest on the beach and immodest at a presidential reception. The first time a daring new fashion appears it may be shocking, but it soon becomes so commonplace as to be almost unnoticed. It would appear that after the first day of observation, the topless beaches on the south coast of France are merely a matter of scenic routine. The ebb and flow of such fashions ought to be dictated more by matters of good taste and common sense (and many fashions past and present showed very little of the latter) and not by moral dicta. There was a time not so long ago when Catholic moral enthusiasts used to try to enforce modesty in dress by providing specific measurements for women's wear (never for menswear, curiously enough). It never occurred to such crusaders that more important to the happiness and holiness of men and women than dressing properly in public before you were married was undressing properly in private after you were married and that crusades for the former might notably inhibit the latter. There are at least some evils from which we have been delivered—though for how long remains to be seen. It is often argued by puritans that "immodest dress" among young women leads young men to have "sinful thoughts." Doubtless bikinis, short shorts, skintight maillots, transparent blouses, strapless gowns, and various other allurements do indeed stir up youthful male passions. But then so would the body of a young woman completely and totally clad. The marginal increment of "immodest thoughts" created by "suggestive" garb is probably minor. Young men who do not have "dirty" thoughts about young women probably need a physical checkup or psychotherapy.

MARRIAGE, DIVORCE, REMARRIAGE

Divorce rates in the United States have gone up in recent years (though in the half-year before the writing of this volume they have leveled off once again). The usual predictions are being made about the decline of the family, predictions which ignore the previous predictions of the same sort that have been proven wrong and that most of those who divorce soon remarry to begin another family. Demographers point out that far more marriages were terminated by death for people in their twenties, thirties, and forties a hundred years ago than are terminated by divorce today. They also observe that in the early part of the last century our ancestors when entering marriage could expect it to last on the average twelve years before one or the other partner died. Now marriages will last on the average four times as long—48 years. The skills of patience, reconciliation, perseverence, excitement, and adventure which are required for such long marriages simply do not seem to abound in the human condition at the present time. Unfortunately the Church is doing little to help people develop such skills. The change in annulment policies discussed elsewhere in this book have enabled the Church to move away from an absolutely rigid insistence on indissolubility (which, of course, was never a total insistence). But little will be accomplished by annulment reform if it is merely a Catholic divorce which if less readily available than Nevada divorces is still reasonably available for many people. The Catholic ideal of permanent commitment of a man and woman to one another is a noble one, and still admired by many who are not Catholic. One need only spend part of one's life in an environment where that ideal, however admired, has no practical operating force to realize that its absence creates even more human suffering than an overrigid insistence on the ideal. The challenge for the Church in the years ahead is to find ways not merely of reenforcing and validating the attractiveness of the ideal but of helping men and women to develop the skills necessary to achieve it. Work in that direction has not even begun.

FAITH-HEALING

There is no reason to deny the sincerity of faith-healers whether they be Protestant or, more recently, Catholics within the charismatic movement. There is also no reason to deny that some psychogenic conditions can be healed permanently or temporarily by faith-healing techniques. Nor is there any reason to doubt that faith-healing methods (intense psychological manipulation) can produce certain short-run physical changes. Finally, it is at least arguable that some bona fide medical cures can be accomplished by faith-healing techniques, though the debate, for example, about the psychological surgeons of the Philippines are filled with very conflicting evidence. Nevertheless, when all these comments are made it is still the case that most faith-healing is fakery—perhaps unintended but fakery nonetheless. Catholics should be profoundly skeptical about claims for such power.

EXCOMMUNICATION

People rarely get thrown out of the Church any more. The last case of excommunication I can remember in the United States was the excommunication of the racist opponents of Catholic school integration in New Orleans by the then gloriously reigning Archbishop John Cody. That excommunication put Catholic liberals in a real bind. They liked to see the book thrown at the racists, but they were dubious about the medieval technique of anathematizing anyone. At the present writing, instead of excommunicating rebel Archbishop Lefebvre the Vatican simply refuses to acknowledge his communications. The Vatican approach is saying that by his behavior Archbishop Lefebvre has removed himself from the ordinary communication links of the Church. It comes to the same thing, of course, but it sounds much more gentle and much less medieval. In reality, certain kinds of actions and behaviors do indeed cause one to sunder the bonds of unity with the Church; but it seems to be a much wiser policy in the present era to simply note that fact instead of issuing a solemn anathema.

CHURCH CENSORSHIP

Remember the Index of Forbidden Books? I'll bet you forgot about it. So, too, has virtually everyone forgotten Church censorship. All at once, without warning and without consultation, American Catholic writers stopped submitting their books for censorship and bishops stopped requiring it. Both sides heaved a sigh of relief. The change was carried out with hardly a public word being said. Chancery offices today are astonished and embarrassed when somebody submits a book for censorship, because it means they have to dig back in the files and find the list of censors. Some religious orders still insist on censorship occasionally, and liturgical and church music publishers have been driven frantic by shifting and changing Church policy on official editions of books used for worship. But the censoring of books and articles both before and after publication seems to have quietly but definitively receded into the past. One need only think of the torment endured by Teilhard de Chardin to realize how ugly and evil the old censorship processes were. We are well rid of them. It is astonishing how quietly they sunk under the sea. A very interesting research project would be to find out how in the United States such a change happened so easily, peacefully, and silently.

CANON LAW

The Church, like every human institution, needs a set of operating procedures, by-laws, ground rules, regulations, processes, norms. One can no more abolish canon law than one can abolish the Church as an institution made up of human beings. The present existing Code of Canon Law (more than 2,000 individual canons) is a monumental codification of disparate canonical sources, many of them centuries old. The Code was issued in 1918, and while it was a marvel of enlightenment for the Church of its day, was outmoded and even dangerously irrelevant within several decades. A new Code of Canon Law was prepared by a commission created by the Vatican Council, and by all accounts it is an absolute disaster—in many ways being even more narrow, rigid, legalistic, and juridical than the old one, and even more out of touch with the needs and problems of contemporary human beings and contemporary Church men and women. (The norms for matrimonial tribunals, which have made annulments possible in the United States, for example, are not included in the new Code.) The Vatican and the code commission are still wheeling and dealing, conniving and maneuvering, hesitating and threatening, guessing and second-guessing about this new code. Most of the practicing canonists of the world are offering prayers and pious works everyday of their lives that the new code will never be issued. Some Americans are afraid that Pope Paul VI might *motu proprio* (on his own initiative) simply end all the controversy over the revised code and proclaim it as the official law of the Church. Many canonists threaten to resign their positions if that does happen, and all seem to agree that it would be the end of all respect for the canonical law tradition (an important and impressive legal tradition, by the way, no matter how deficient it may be in its present manifestation). The best sources in Rome, however, suggest that it will be many more years before the new code is promulgated (if it ever is). There is still hope, then, that a simplified, flexible, sensitive restructuring of the canon law tradition might be possible.

SHRINES AND PILGRIMAGES

Pilgrimages to great religious shrines (Lourdes, Walsingham, Fatima, the National Shrine of the Immaculate Conception in Washington, Guadalupe, St. James Campostela) have notably declined since the Vatican council, right? Wrong. Pilgrimages and shrines are in not out, and more pilgrims came to Rome in the most recent Holy Year than for any previous one. (My guess is that most of the married folks that came to the Holy Year carried their birth control devices in their purses.) Holy places are still important to human beings, and making trips to them is still an act of devotion (though since Chaucer we realize that lots of other things besides devotion happen on pilgrimages). Highbrow liturgists and theologians are appalled and aghast at this shrine/pilgrimage phenomenon and do their best to pretend that it doesn't happen. Sociologists and historians of religion, on the other hand, are not surprised—or at least they shouldn't be. The notion that some places are sacred or holy in a unique and special way has been with the human race since the beginning of religion. One goes to such places because one encounters there in an extraordinary way *the* holy, that is to say, the tremendous, fascinating, the awesome. Many liturgists and theologians apparently would like all sense of awe and the sacred to go out of life. After all, we have been "secularized," haven't we? The truth is, to quote a phrase, we are still "unsecular man."* Only those with the most naive and simple-minded, unidirectional concepts of the evolution of humankind from the sacred to the secular will be surprised at the survival of holy places and of journeyings to those places. There is now a tendency among Americans in particular to reevaluate folk religion—though to use it as part of *la revolution*. It might be appropriate if elite Church scholars, figures, and pontificators began to reevaluate the importance of sacred place and sacred time in the lives of ordinary people.

* See *Unsecular Man* by Andrew M. Greeley (New York: Schocken, 1972). Obviously, if I had it to do over again I would have called the book "Unsecular Humankind." You've probably read the book, but you might want to look at it again.

NOVENAS

The Novena is a popular devotion involving the number nine—nine days, nine first Fridays, etc. The idea was that there was something magic or quasi-magic about the number nine. If you did the holy thing nine times, you were working both sides of the fence; you had both the holy and the magic going for you. In Chicago, during the Great Depression, tens of thousands of people waited outside on Jackson Blvd. in front of Our Lady of Sorrows Church (now Our Lady of Sorrows Basilica, and mostly unoccupied because of the changing neighborhood in which the church is located) to participate in the Novena of the Sorrowful Mother. "Post-Vatican Catholics" tend to look down on the old novenas (and they often were pretty gruesome) and the novena-goers. While there was doubtless much inadequate in the style of the novena piety, it is nonetheless true that many people did use the novena as a means of expressing authentic religiousness and devotion at a time when there was almost nothing else available in their own language with which they could offer public prayer. Heaven knows, more people went to the novenas than went to the now moribund "bible vigils" of the 1960s. (I'm told that young priests coming out of the seminary are pushing vespers again. Sometimes we never learn!) It is interesting to observe, incidentally, that the only change in the Post-Vatican Church that Catholics disapproved of, as shown by the NORC study of American Catholics, was the decline in non-

liturgical devotions. Most Catholics in the age of
television, heaven knows, didn't attend them, but
they think that such devotions still ought to be available
to those who want them.

ROSARY

A form of marian devotion which flourished for
hundreds of years and was finally killed off by the
hypersaccharin piety of the professional mariologists
and the compulsiveness of many grammar school
teachers. Given a quarter of a century, maybe less,
lots of folk will argue that the rosary is an attractive
objet d'art and a prayer form comparable with many
of the most honored eastern prayer practices. You
never know what's in fashion and what's out.

GREGORIAN CHANT

An immensely important music form in which many works of great musical genius have been produced and according to which the Church sang its public worship for a thousand years and more. It was killed off by bad instruction, poor singing, and horrendous clerical education even before the vernacular liturgy arrived. One hears very little Gregorian chant in church these days, in part because a whole generation of priests, religious, and laity came to hate it, and in part because Gregorian purists insisted that you cannot write plainsong to accompany English lyrics. (Plainsong was almost certainly Greek in origin and doubtless there were purists who claimed you could not use it to accompany Latin hymns.) It is one more treasure of the Christian heritage that the compulsive rigidity of the right and the doctrinaire shallowness of the left has temporarily obliterated. Gregorian chant records still sell quite well in music stores, however; we will almost certainly see a plainsong revival sometime in the near future. Like I say, so it goes.

GENETIC ENGINEERING

One of few intelligent statements issued by the American hierarchy in recent years dealt with the subject of DNA experiments,* stated the general principles of respect for the integrity of human life, presented both sides of the argument (the dangers of messing with DNA on the one hand versus the extraordinary advances that may be possible on the other), and concluded by urging scientists to work out this problem as best they could in collaboration with the public, realizing that it is not merely a problem of science but also one of ethics, morality, and religion. The resolute refusal of the committee to come down on one side or the other of the controversy when all the facts are not in was surely commendable, especially because such restraint is very rare in the clergy and the hierarchy these days. There are some enthusiastic geneticists who do not want to permit people with color-blindness genes or diabetes genes or sickle-cell anemia genes to have children on the grounds that such reproduction weakens the gene pool and increases the social cost of children born with such "defective" genes. As one who would not have been permitted to enter the world if such laws existed a half-century ago, I am understandably appalled that people would even think them. Doubt-

* "Statement on Recombinant DNA Research," Bishop's Committee for Human Values, U.S. Catholic Conference, Washington, D.C., May 1977.

less one can selectively breed flowers, grain, and cattle for special characteristics, but we do not have even the beginnings of information of how to breed the human race selectively to provide a better species even if we could agree on what would constitute a better species. Furthermore, it is not at all clear that we would want to or ought to improve it by selective breeding, for there are other and substantially more important questions in choosing one's spouse or deciding to have children than genetic characteristics. However, one should never underestimate the persistence and determination of some of the genetic manipulation crowd. Given half a chance they may well impose their half-mad theories on the rest of us. Impossible, you say? So would have seemed the discrimination against white men simply because they are white men just a quarter century ago.

BENEDICTION OF THE BLESSED SACRAMENT

A popular devotion which was not all that popular but which used to mark such things as graduations, church dedications, confirmations, and other celebrations in the Church—mostly because you could do it in English. The Eucharist, more appropriately and more fittingly, has replaced the benediction at these functions now. Some older folk still like it, and some younger folk find it interesting and amusing; there is nothing wrong with doing it occasionally, but it is one form of popular piety that is unlikely to recur—largely because there is no functional need for it. That does not mean, however, that we do not need a good, solid, extraliturgical public devotion which is less solemn than mass and quicker and also "low churchish" than the bible vigil. The winner of a contest to come up with such a popular devotion should receive a round trip ticket to the shrine of his choice.

ORGAN TRANSPLANTS

I don't think anyone has any particular problem with organ transplants anymore. There may be some problem about how you go about collecting the organ. (I think some doctors even use the word "harvesting" the organ, God help us!) It is a complicated moral and medical problem, for example, as to when a person is sufficiently dead so that removing his heart is not murder. This one is beyond me, but that doesn't mean it's unimportant. Consult your favorite moral medical specialist if you're really interested.

FREE WILL

The capacity to be responsible for our own decisions and acts. At one time Catholics seemed to think that virtually everything we did was a matter of free will choice, whereas non-Catholic intellectuals thought rather the opposite. There has been a gradual convergence in the two positions with Catholics recognizing that complete or even minimal freedom is absent from many human activities and the agnostics grudgingly conceding in practice if not in theory that there may be such a thing as freedom of choice.

NECKING AND PETTING

Love play involving fondling, kissing, caressing—
sometimes quite vigorous indeed. It was once the
favorite outdoor sport of American teenagers after
age 16, which was roundly denounced by the Church
as a horrendous sin on the grounds that (a) it involved sexual pleasure outside of marriage and (b) it
inevitably led to intercourse. The kids responded that
(a) "it's fun!" and (b) in their experience it rarely if
ever led to intercourse (unless they were engaged).
Many teachers, preachers, priests, and parents would
rejoice if kids today just stopped with necking and
petting instead of jumping into bed together after the
second date. Modern birth control technology makes
jumping into bed as safe physically as necking and
petting was a couple of decades ago. It is not nearly
so safe psychologically, but the youth culture conven-
tional wisdom doesn't realize that, and college psychological counselors, always afraid of being labeled
"old fashioned," don't tell young people that with
sufficient vigor. The real human problem, however, is
not so much necking and petting before marriage but
not enough after it. There is too much fear, anger,
disillusionment, and cool romantic ardor.

DIRTY THOUGHTS

Erotic thoughts, once a routine matter for confession for Catholics and still frequently heard from those who continue to go to confession. It used to be said that erotic thoughts were sinful only if you enjoyed them, but as one clergyman observed, "What's the use of having such thoughts unless they're enjoyable?" In fact, one can no more avoid erotic thoughts if one is a healthy member of the human race with one's endocrine glands in proper working order than one can avoid pollen by walking through a field in late August. They are psychologically, spiritually, or religiously harmful only when they become obsessive or when they interfere with one's fundamental life commitments.

HELL, LIMBO, PURGATORY

Limbo has pretty much gone down the drain. It was a compromise dreamed up because St. Augustine, with reckless consistency, was willing to permit unbaptized infants to go to Hell. More recently, theologians have realized that that idea was an aberration of Augustine's troubled personality and not sound doctrine. Jesus came to make salvation available to all, and however Augustine might try to justify it, it simply would not be just to confine to Hell, or even to deny a chance for Heaven, infants who were incapable of receiving baptism for one reason or another. Purgatory is a much more reasonable and consoling doctrine. It is a place where we can "catch up" on the growing, on the preparation we didn't get a chance to do on earth. Hell is a tough one, for to deny the existence of Hell means to deny the importance of human freedom and to reduce the choices we make during our lifetimes to irrelevancy. One can forget about the hellfire, the sulphur, the Dantesque imagery; one still must acknowledge, it seems, the possibility of loss, of self-chosen isolation, alienation, separation. Whether such folk get another chance or not is something best left to the mercy of God.

SALVATION OUTSIDE THE CHURCH

It is certainly the case that you cannot be saved if you recognize that the Catholic Church is the one true church and consciously, deliberately, and maliciously refuse to join it. How many people, if any, have ever done that seems problematic. In any case, anyone who explicitly and deliberately turns his back on truth, goodness, and beauty has committed grave sin. Rejection of a church by those who are convinced of its authenticity is simply a species of that sin. God, of course, speaks to all men in all places, and offers all the gift of his loving life. This is precisely what Jesus came to reveal, to validate, and confirm in a unique, special, and extraordinary way. One can say, of course, that all those who respond positively to the invitation that life offers them for goodness and love are in some fashion part of the Church because they are part of God's people (even if they don't realize it). In some sense this answer would be theologically true, though many non-Catholics would find it offensive if phrased precisely that way. It would be better to say that God offers life to all, and those who accept the offer are God's friends forever. To make them non-voting and unconscious members of the *Ecclesia Catolica Sancta Romana* may be a form of theological gerrymandering and just a bit too much. It should be sufficient for Catholics to say that, all things considered, they believe their religious commitment to be the most authentic, the most adequate, and the fullest response to God's love for them.

LIFE IN OUTER SPACE

It seems most unlikely that life, so prodigal on this earth, would be limited to this earth. So it should not be surprising to find sentient life, and even rational life, scattered all over the cosmos. Whether it will be rational life like ours is a question of great fascination, one on which the science fiction industry relies heavily. Some Catholic authors used to suggest that it would be impossible for there to be rational life elsewhere in the universe unless in some way or the other it was related to the "economy" of salvation worked out here on earth. That was theological geocentrism with a vengeance. Alice Maynell much more appropriately wondered in a beautiful poem, "in what shape Christ would walk the Pleiades." Some folks seem to think that Christians ought to be terribly worried that life in outer space would be a threat to the faith. One cannot imagine why it should be; it seems much more reasonable to wait eagerly to find out what wonders our wild, manic God has thought up for other planets.

JUST WAR

Catholic ethical theory has traditionally argued that certain kinds of war were not immoral—wars in self-defense, for example, when the good was not exceeded by the harm. More recently, some Catholics have argued that given the advent of nuclear weapons, there can no longer be a just war, and that pacifism can be the only Christian response. It is easy to argue such a position when the American nuclear umbrella keeps one out of a communist concentration camp. The pacifist position is beautiful in its logic, its neatness, and simplicity; but like all simple, logical, beautiful, and neat moral stances, it does not take into sufficient account the complexities of the human condition. There are times, regrettably, when one must fight to defend those things and those persons which are critically important. It is to be hoped that one fights without vengeance, without hatred, without vindictiveness; and only after all other measures have been tried.

REVOLUTION

Catholic ethical theory has traditionally recognized the right of political revolution. Indeed, it was more likely to recognize the right of revolution than Renaissance Protestant or modern agnostic political theory. However, it recognizes the legitimacy of revolution only under extreme circumstances and only when all other lesser measures have failed. Some contemporary Catholic thinkers have become "macho" on the subject of revolution, as though one only achieves validation, legitimacy, and authenticity by becoming part of "la revolucion." It seems to give some Catholics a vicarious thrill to talk about revolution— all the fun of being a terrorist without any of the risks. One must say that talk about revolution comes cheap from tenured university and college faculty members. It is also odd that those who advocate revolution most enthusiastically are also precisely those who are pacifists on the subject of a "just war." They also are the ones who call on the clergy to lead revolutions in Latin America but are appalled when the clergy do not denounce revolutions in Northern Ireland, who criticize Richard Daley for sending money to aid Northern Ireland, but don't criticize the World Council of Churches for sending money for revolutions to black guerillas in South Africa—but in Ireland it's senseless barbarism. (I suspect it would be if the Lithuanians started revolting, too.) I remember sitting in a meeting of European scholars who were passionately discussing political theology, revolutionary theology, liberation theology beneath the great, gray Victorian walls of St. Patrick's Seminary, Maynooth, County Kildare, Ireland. I repeatedly suggested that we had some real revolutionaries not too far away and could probably find some Sinn Feiners in the nearest pub. Might it not be appropriate, I suggested, to bring in some revolutionaries to join the discussion? Finally, one German academic bureaucrat shouted me down. "The war in Ulster," he announced, "is not a people's struggle for freedom." I still haven't been able to figure out what—in his mind—the hell it was.

AUTHORSHIP OF THE BIBLE

The bible is a collection of books written, for the most part, between 400 B.C. and 100 A.D. by Jewish and Jewish-Christian authors. It contains the accounts of God's special words and deeds in dealing with the Jewish people down through the ages and with the early followers of Jesus of Nazareth. In the sense that the bible is an account of God's deeds, an account which is in a profoundly fundamental way accurate and faithful in its recording of God's deeds, God can surely be said to be its author. (In a way he is not, let us say, the author of Tolstoy's *War and Peace*.) But God is not responsible for St. Matthew's Greek, St. Paul's grammar, for the Pentateuch tradition's notion of science and cosmology, or even for the early Christian's expectation for an imminent end of the world. I have the impression that not many Catholics worry about this one any more, and that's just as well. The religious symbols developed, expanded, reinterpreted, enriched, and authenticated in the bible are of immense importance to our lives. It is far better for us to try to understand the implications of these symbols than to engage in arid, dry, and pointless debates about whether God was the author of the punctuation marks in St. John's text.

DIACONATE

An early Christian clerical office first described in Jerusalem in the Acts of the Apostles concerned mostly with ecclesiastical administration. In a later stage in Rome, it was the deacon and not the priest who was likely to be elected pope, because he had to be an administrator; a deacon was thought to be more skilled and experienced at such matters. Later on, the diaconate was merged with the priesthood and became a formal stepping stone to it. Recently, a permanent diaconate (badly named, of course, because those priests who were once deacons still have the power of the diaconal office) has been established mostly for married men who in the present discipline are unable to become priests. Curiously enough, the permanent deacons (sometimes even called, more appallingly, "lay deacons") do exactly the opposite of the deacons in the early church. The last thing in the world the parish clergy are willing to do is to trust their deacons with parish finances. The problem in the present revitalization of the diaconate is that it has not been thought through with sufficient clarity and is frequently still conceptualized as simply one more form of lay apostolate. "I don't want them wearing Roman collars," said one pastor. "The laity will start to think they're clergy." I didn't tell the poor man that they were every bit as much clergy as he was, in part, because de facto, they are not thought of as clergy by the laity or permitted to do clerical things, whatever their canonical and sacramental status may be. They are in fact second-class clergy who are permitted some role in the Church because we can't have married priests.

LAY APOSTOLATE

The very sensible notion that most of the work of the Church cannot be done by the clergy, that in particular the clergy are unsuited, untrained, and unequipped to witness God's love as manifested in Christ in the arenas of daily life and work. The lay apostolate does not mean that laity vote on parish councils, keep parish books, or run parish athletic programs; it means primarily that the laity witness to the truth the Church proclaims in the world in which they live and work. (Though, of course, lay involvement in the affairs of the ecclesiastical institution is surely proper, necessary, and essential.) The lay apostolate was a very heavy thing in the Church in America between 1945 and 1965, but it kind of got wiped out when most of the folks who supported it discovered that all their dreams had become true at the Vatican Council and the world and the Church were still left imperfect. The theory of "like to like," however, on which the lay apostolate was based is theologically, psychologically, and sociologically sound. If there was anything wrong with the various Cardijn movements (named after Canon, later Cardinal, Cardijn, the Belgian who began the Young Christian Workers), it was that they had entirely too

107

simplistic a notion of the spiritual "formation" (by which was meant training and support) required of those who take their commission, indeed their ordination (from the sacrament of baptism), to the lay apostolate seriously.

EASTERN RITE

The Roman Catholic Church, most of us know, is more than just Roman. There are Syrian, Maronite, Syro-malabar, Syro-malenkar, Coptic, Greek Ukrainian, Ruthenian, and a host of others who maintain some form or other of unity with Rome but have their own customs, practices, liturgies, doctrinal formulations, and canon law. These folks are usually treated like poor cousins by Roman Catholics (in the United States, they have even been forbidden to continue their practice of a married clergy) and generally get pushed around. On the other hand, they are often difficult, touchy, folks (not altogether without reason). They are also, in some sense, a barrier to ecumenism because the Orthodox Christians look on the Uniates as sellouts to Rome, as descendants of people who converted to Rome under pressure or for political or personal gain. Exactly what would happen to the Uniate rite should the Orthodox churches come back into communion with Rome is not clear. Presumably, they would simply continue as separate "denominations" within the large unity and would live in somewhat greater peace with their Orthodox counterparts than they do now. It is sometimes, in the United States, at least, very hard to tell who is Uniate and who is Orthodox, because parishes move in and out and about with bewildering ease and speed. We members of the Roman rite should avoid patronizing our Eastern rite brothers and sisters and strive to learn from the riches of their traditions—without of course, denying the riches of our own.

GENERAL ABSOLUTION

The pronouncement of the key component of the sacrament of penance to a large group of people without the personal confession of sins. At present it is permitted in cases of necessity or emergency. When an American bishop argued that the presence of a large crowd of people constituted such an emergency, he was briskly rebuked by Rome. His mistake was to do it in public. All kinds of priests and even some bishops have awarded general absolution privately, and no one is the worse for it. Rome does permit general absolution services under some circumstances when private confession has taken place beforehand (but then what is the point of a general absolution?). Many priests have general absolution services privately, in part because of the notable decline in reception of the sacrament of penance in recent years. Hopefully, we can develop a practice in which the values of both general absolution services and private confession will be maintained and available to all who seek them. Such practice would certainly be much better than the gross abuse of the sacraments that was widespread in the American Church not so long ago when on the Thursday before First Friday, all school children were herded into the church and compelled to go to confession. (Thank God that doesn't happen any more—though in some dioceses, young people are in fact being compelled to go to confession before first communion, which is certainly an abuse of the sacrament whether Rome insists on it or not.) It must be said honestly, however, that here as in so many other areas of contemporary Catholic life, the possibilities of a flexible, multi-faceted, pluralistic penitential discipline have not even begun to be realized, in part because of Roman obscurantism and in part because of theological impasses and sloth.

RAPE

The violent sexual abuse of another person. An evil, ugly, horrendous sin, most frequently the abuse of a woman by a man. (Though down through human history it has been by no means the only kind of rape.) Rape is usually a raw, primal action which occurs simply because the man is physically stronger than a woman and can dominate her. Members of the feminist movement quite properly point out that some forms of marital intercourse are in fact very little better than legalized rape. Most often rape is not even sexual behavior as much as it is a form of satisfaction gained from physical violence, domination, and cruelty. Nor is the chauvinistic double-standard argument that women bring rape on themselves by acting seductively a legitimate excuse at all. The rapist needs no invitation. On the other hand, feminine activists like Susan Brownmuller are wrong when they try to interpret the whole history of the relationship between the sexes in terms of rape and claim that all men are rapists or at least sympathizers with rape. No such simplistic interpretation of sexuality or history serves any useful purpose. All these points having been made, it must still be noted (in case the reader's fantasy life has not made it obvious to him/her) that sexual intercourse is a vigorous, not to say violent, activity; and even in the most loving exchange there is an element of taking and yielding, of conquering and surrendering, of dominating and being overwhelmed (with man and woman playing both roles in a healthy, happy relationship). Resistance (from either partner) is sometimes serious, sometimes half-serious, and sometimes part of the adventure. Well-adjusted couples develop a set of signals, codes by which they indicate which sort of resistance they are offering one another. In a wise, sensitive relationship, this code is honored and respected. To be forced to make love against one's will is in some cases a horrible degradation, in others merely heightens the pleasure and the joy of the love-making. It all depends on which meaning is being attached to the forced, "against one's will" signal. Sometimes it means, "I really do mean 'leave me alone.'" Other times it means, "I don't much care, but if you want to, maybe you can make me care." Still other times it means, "Today I really need some-one strong, masterful, powerful, dominating. Be that someone and sweep me off my feet." Both the man and the woman, of course, should be able to send up such signals to one another. It is a vile and dangerous temptation to change the meaning of the signal in the middle of the game in order to punish the other.

SHROUD OF TURIN

I don't care much whether the Holy Shroud of Turin is indeed the cloth in which Jesus was wrapped in the holy sepulcher. It may be an interesting historical question, but religiously it belongs in the same category as do relics, tombs, basements full of skulls, ashes on Ash Wednesday, and the *Dies Irae*— morbid, medieval, and not altogether Christian. But if it's your thing, go buy a book on it. Don't expect to learn anything from me on the subject. It's a pluralistic church and you're entitled to your Shroud of Turin if you want it.

CHRISTIAN BURIAL/ CREMATION

Christians, along with their Jewish cousins, insisted on the burial of the dead during the time of the Roman empire because the Roman practice of cremation seemed to bespeak a denial of the resurrection; also, perhaps, because burial showed greater respect for those physical remains which were once the seat of the human personality and which would be again someday. Of course, decomposition in the tomb is merely a longer process than that which takes place in the crematorium. The Church vigorously resisted cremation "save in times of plague and other disasters." It has recently modified its opposition somewhat. However, in the minds of many people cremation still hints strongly at denial of the resurrection, so the Church responds by insisting that for both doctrinal and historical reasons that in the ordinary set of circumstances, burial is the appropriate way of disposing of the body in which there was once life and for which there is hope of life once again.

MIRACLES AND APPARITIONS

It is an open universe. Only the crudest and most rigid of mechanical interpretations of the cosmos exclude the possibility of the wonderful and the marvelous. If it was wrong for some Catholics to turn their religion into what was little more than a cult of the miracle and the private revelation, it was equally wrong and narrow for agnostics to insist that the universe could only operate according to already discovered scientific laws. The miracles of the New Testament, we now know, are not proofs but rather signs designed to stir up wonder and surprise. (Scripture scholars agree today that (a) most of our miracle texts are theological stories, (b) the tradition of Jesus being a wonder worker is too ancient and too strong not to represent some historical reality, and (c) the miracle stories in the New Testament are discreet, modest, and unspectacular compared to the standard set by other religious tales of the same era.) The proper attitude toward such marvels when they are reported is profound skepticism, because most miracles and apparitions are the product of troubled, disturbed personalities; on the other hand, the wise person keeps an open mind, realizing that there are far more things under heaven than those for which our science provides adequate explanations. Indeed, the refusal of science to take wonders and marvels seriously is as bad as the refusal of some Catholics to understand that the marvelous is not the core of the Catholic religious heritage.

MORALITY

Properly speaking, the Catholic Church is not in the morality business at all despite the impression most of us got when we were growing up. The Church is in the religion business, and religion and morality—again despite our impressions—are not the same thing. Both are practical theories, not speculative like philosophy; both deal with how one lives. But religion explains the ultimate purposes of human life and of the existence of the cosmos of which we are a part. Religion tells us whether it's safe to hope, to trust, to take chances, to seriously accept the primal thrust of the human personality toward the conviction that life does have a purpose that transcends itself and that it is safe to love. Morality is a system of principles covering the day-to-day choices between good and evil humankind must make. Religion tells us that the world and its processes are ultimately good (or perhaps evil); morality tells us what kind of human behavior is good. The two are obviously related, because one's decisions about the nature of the universe and the purposes of human life create the context in which moral choices must be made; but many people with different visions of the ultimate purpose of human life can still agree on fundamental moral principles, because the consequences of human behavior are the same no matter what one's ultimate worldview. Neither Jesus nor St. Paul were systematic ethicians; they were rather prophets (in Jesus' case, of course, more than prophet), teachers of religion, expounders of a worldview, men who claimed to have a vision of who God was and why he created us. Both, indeed, vigorously resisted the hyperlegalization of the Jewish ethical theory in the environment in which they lived. Neither hesitated to offer moral advice to their followers, but moral concerns were secondary to religious ones. Christian thinkers after the time of Jesus and St. Paul and the other apostles developed a specific moral heritage in which the traditional wisdom of the Greek, Roman, and Hebrew moral thinkers was reformulated to some considerable extent in light of the Christian insights about the meaning of the world and the meaning of human life. This Christian morality was derived from twin sources, the gospel and the philosophic systems of the early eras and then subsequent eras. Obviously the Christian moral theory must be taken very seriously by those who claim to be followers of Jesus of Nazareth because it is the only one that claims to be illumined by the revelation of the nature of God that was contained in the life, death, and resurrection of Jesus. (Of course, within the Christian moral system there are many different traditions.) Most of this book is concerned with moral questions rather than religious questions in the strict sense of the word.* Moral questions are important; they are less important than religious questions. They are also easier to answer and easier to live by. It is much

* For religious questions, see my book *The Great Mysteries: An Essential Catechism* (New York: Seabury Press, 1977).

easier to keep the law than to respond enthusiastically and generously to the passionate love of God which was revealed in Jesus. Unfortunately for the legalist in all of us, Jesus made it very clear that it was passionate love he required, not merely moral obedience.

CATHOLIC SOCIAL THEORY

The traditional teaching of the Catholic Church on the nature of human society, a perspective which the Church shares with many other groups such as the Buddhists and that stream of Anglo-Saxon legal thinking which produced the American Republic. Catholic social theory rejects both capitalism and socialism on the grounds that these two views of the nature of human society are too individualistic. They view the individual as entering societal relationships as an isolated atom either struggling for his own enlightened self-interest, as in the case of capitalism, or as being remade into a generous socially concerned "new man" in socialism. In fact, according to the Catholic social theory, society is not a collection of isolated individuals but rather a dense organic network of many groups, formal and informal. Humans act in society not as isolated individuals but as members of communities, large and small, communities which must be respected by any larger social structure, especially the state. There are three cardinal principles in Catholic social theory:

(1) *Personalism.* Both society and its formal institutions of the state exist to enhance the welfare of the individual person and not vice versa. The person is not a pawn at the mercy of the state and society; the person is the goal of society.

(2) *Pluralism.* The healthy society is composed of many different groups, communities, institutions, relational networks, self-help organizations all relatively autonomous and independent, and all with the rights and privileges of a free, self-governing existence within the larger society. While a pluralistic society may be messy, complicated, difficult to analyze and chart, it responds much more appropriately to the complexities of the human condition and human nature than the tightly organized, rigid, inflexible, bureaucratic societies of both capitalism and socialism.

(3) *Subsidiarity (or decentralization).* Catholic social theory is convinced that nothing should be done by a larger and higher level organization than can be done equally as well by a smaller and lower level organization. *Small is beautiful,* according to the convert/author E. F. Schumacher, and every institution should be *No larger than necessary,* according to another book of mine. The bureaucratic state, whether it be capitalist or socialist, preaches centralization and giantism; the Catholic social theory preaches decentralization and as much smallness, as much independence, as much neighborhood or local community control as possible.

While Catholic social theory has a long and glorious tradition, and while its principles are being discovered again by many non-Catholics today, most contemporary Catholic social theorists have abandoned it for a mixture of Protestant guilt, liberal-left cliches, and warmed-over Marxism. The new catechetical directory of the American hierarchy, for example, does not mention subsidiarity once in a several thousand word review of Catholic social theory. Nor does it mention localism, communalism, pluralism, or neighborhoods.

THE TRINITY

The Catholic Christian religious symbol which indicates that God is relational in an ongoing process of knowledge and love. In the old days we thought of the Trinity as a bafflement to test our faith. Recently we discovered the fact that mysteries aren't dark puzzles to torment us but dazzling shafts of light which blind us by their brilliance. The mystery of the triune God is the mystery of God as relational process, God as ongoing knowledge and love.

MISSIONS AND MISSIONARIES

Christianity, like Judaism of the Second Temple era, had a powerful missionary impulse. Some scholars think that anywhere from one-sixth to one-quarter of the urban dwellers of the Roman Empire were Jews or Jewish proselytes. After the fall of the temple, rabbinic Judaism turned away from missionary activity for the most part. The command of Jesus to preach the Good News to the ends of the earth has been taken very seriously indeed by Christians ever since. In the eighteenth, nineteenth, and twentieth centuries, with the opening up of the world and the development of rapid means of transportation and communication, there was a tremendous surge of missionary activity. Men and women went unselfishly and enthusiastically to virtually every country in the world to organize the Catholic Church. Unfortunately but inevitably, both in the minds of the missionaries and in the minds of the natives, Christianity became identified with Western European culture, and the revolt of the "Third World" nations against Western domination (though in terms of Western political theory and with the aid of Western technology) the missionaries were left very vulnerable. Many of them began to think of themselves as "the foreign devils" their opponents called them and turned from proclaiming the Good News of the gospel to political action as a form of "preevangelization," preparing the way in the social and economic environment for the preaching of the gospel. The missionary impulse seems to have waned recently. There are fewer missionary occasions, more anguish and self-doubt among the missionaries and more obscurity in their thinking about the relationship between the political and the religious. The early Christian missionaries had no trouble adapting the gospels to the cultural environment in which they found themselves—be it Gaul, Ireland, Germany, or the Slavonic countries of Eastern Europe. Later on, however, the identification between Christianity and Europe became so definitive that adaptation was forbidden—most notably in the experiments of Matteo Ricci in China and Roberto di Nobili in India. It is now clear to virtually everyone that the missionaries should be speaking for the gospel of Jesus and not for Western civilization; but the problem is made more complicated by the fact that even the most militant nationalists in the Third World countries are themselves products of Western education. The missionary orders are trying to rethink the meaning of the missionary impulse in light of the shattering experiences of the last half-century. It must be said that thus far their attempts to reformulate their role have been less than success-ful—possibly because many of the theorists no longer seem to think that proclaiming the Good News of the gospel in language that others can understand is all that important.

AQUINAS

A thirteenth-century Dominican theologian, perhaps the greatest Catholic thinker in all history, done-in in the middle of the twentieth century by his own adherents, who rigidly supported the letter of what he said and ignored the spirit. Aquinas was a flexible, creative innovator who salvaged Aristotle from the Islamic philosophers who brought him to Europe from Spain and created a synthesis between Greek realistic philosophy and Christianity which still dominates the basic assumptions of Catholic teaching and has had immense impact on the rest of the Western world. His books were burned at Oxford and he himself was condemned in Paris (after his death) precisely because he was too flexible, too innovative, too willing to take intellectual risks. Many of those who claim to be Thomists in this century are utterly devoid of such characteristics. Yet some of the best Catholic theology currently being done—Bernard Lonergan and David Tracy and Karl Rahner, for example—are proud to call themselves Thomists.

AUGUSTINE

A Western Catholic thinker of the fifth-century who developed the most elaborate synthesis of platonic philosophical theory and Christian religious symbols. Augustine was a brilliant, tormented, convoluted, complex, erratic man. He left the West with some enduring intellectual tools—the idea of evolutionary progress, conflict between grace and nature, the debate over whether humankind is basically good or evil, pessimism about the human body and particularly about human sexuality. As Aquinas is the Catholic Realist, Augustine is the Catholic Idealist. In many respects the Reformation was an Augustinian revolt against the Aristotelian Middle Ages, a revolt of the dialectical, pessimistic disciples of Augustine against the organic, ontological, relatively optimistic disciplines of Aquinas. The fundamental challenge of Christian theology since the thirteenth century has been not so much creating a synthesis between Augustine and Aquinas as learning how to maintain the two major streams of Christian philosophical thinking in relative harmony one with another. One can see such conflict going on everywhere when one is sensitized to it. Thus the debate within Catholic social theory as to whether Catholic social actionists should be concerned with the maintenance of organic communities like neighborhoods against destructive bureaucratization of urban life (an Aristotelian concern worthy of the disciples of Aquinas) or whether Catholic social theory should be stressing guilt and expiation for the oppression of blacks, American Indians, and the Third World (an Augustinian response). It is all well and good to say that both responses are appropriate and should be balanced; it is maintaining the balance both in practice and in theory that is the art.

EUTHANASIA

The Karen Quinlan case surfaced an anomaly in contemporary moral life. The Quinlans, practicing Catholics and with the advice of their clergy and bishop, were perfectly prepared to pull the plug on the life support mechanisms that artificially kept their daughter alive. It took journalists a long time to grasp that on this aspect of the euthanasia question, at any rate, the Catholic Church was more liberal than the American court system and more liberal than many Protestant churches. On the one hand, Catholic moral theory teaches that one cannot do anything directly to kill the sick, the aged, or the suffering. On the other hand, Catholic moral theory also insists that it is not necessary to use extraordinary means to sustain life in those who are terminally ill, and the withdrawal of these extraordinary means is not murder. Since modern medicine is rather strongly committed to the use of every possible resource to sustain life no matter how futile the exercise may be, in this respect the Catholic moral theory is more "liberal" than is the medical profession. It is very difficult, however, for the Church to keep its faithful members well informed on the nuances of the differences between the direct killing of a patient and permitting him to die by withdrawing extraordinary life support systems. As medical science becomes more sophisticated at keeping us alive even when there is no further purpose in being kept alive, the conflict between the Church's teaching and medical science may grow more intense. On the other hand, the Church cannot make common cause with those euthanasia supporters who view distinctions between direct killing and the withdrawal of life support systems as a meaningless distinction. The dilemma of the Church in this area is likely to get much worse before it gets better.

DEATHBED CONVERSIONS

Dramatic returns to the Church or equally dramatic conversions to the Church in the last moments of life were once hailed as great signs of mercy, the power of God's grace, and of the victory of Catholicism. They are, however, rather difficult to harmonize with the "fundamental option" (QV) approach to Christian life. If your fundamental option has been bad, it might be argued, what good does a deathbed conversion do? Some clergy are not especially concerned about running off in the middle of the night to administer the sacraments of the sick to those who are at death's door (or who have already died) on the grounds that the deathbed conversion approach is more magical than anything else. If the fundamental option has been positive, you don't need a deathbed conversion; if it has been negative, it won't do you much good. However, such an attitude restricts the Holy Spirit as much as did the opposite attitude. God's Spirit blows whither he will; his mercy and grace are beyond human calculation. It is not up to us to judge what a person's fundamental option was or how deathbed events may effect the "story" of a person's life. Human existence simply cannot be stretched to fit academic notions. There is surely no reason to believe that the absence of a deathbed conversion means that the Holy Spirit has been at work. On the other hand, the presence of a deathbed conversion is surely an encouraging sign for the family and friends as well as for the dying person himself.

THE HOLY SPIRIT

That "person" of the divine triad which represents variety, diversity, pluralism. St. Paul says the Spirit speaks to our spirit, meaning that the principle of variety in God speaks to that which is most unique, most special, most authentically us. When we respond to the Spirit with that which is most particularly ourself, we become most individuated, most unique, most special; and thus, in our own way, make the world a more variegated and more diversified place. Even those who most enthusiastically proclaim themselves devotees of the Holy Spirit would frequently want to restrict his freedom of operation and eliminate the variety and diversity in human life and human religious behavior.

ANTIPOPES

At the Council of Basel at the end of the fourteenth century the Catholic Church managed to work its way out of the antipope problem finally. (Though scholars still debate as to who was pope and who was antipope during the great western schism.) There are always a fair number of lunatics dashing around in white garb claiming to be pope (we have a couple even in the city of Chicago), but antipopes seem to cause serious trouble for the Church no longer. One does hear rumors occasionally, however, that the Avignon line of the papacy continues; periodically, somewhere in a small town in France, Avignon cardinals get together and elect a new pope, who promptly cedes jurisdiction for the good of the Church to the antipope in Rome. I've often thought that one could do a perfectly splendid novel on the subject, but I suppose the French have already done that. I don't suppose there is any need at this time to explain antipopes as a "problem to the faith." If there is, see "Bad Popes" in this book.

LITURGICAL CHANGES

Despite what you may read occasionally by liberal Catholic authors, American Catholics overwhelmingly accept the liturgical changes of the Vatican Council. The principal criticism seems to be not of the English liturgy or liturgical change but of badly done liturgy, a problem which will be with us until such time as the Church is ready to make a serious commitment to spending money on the hiring and maintenance of professional Church musicians. One problem the new liturgy does cause (particularly when it is done with some skill) is to make the abysmal poverty of American Catholic sermons even more evident. The quality of sermons has been demonstrated to be the strongest predictor available of people's satisfaction with their parishes. Still, one detects very little effort among the American clergy to upgrade the quality of their sermons.

SACRAMENTS

The sacrament is a symbolic ritual celebrating the union between God and his Church, Christ and his people, making present in a special and appropriate way the saving love of God for particular situations of human life. Sacraments are, above all, signs, explosive indicators that God's loving graciousness is at work. When the sign is shown badly—a poorly said mass, a hastily mumbled baptism, a shuffling confirmation, a tasteless marriage ceremony, the presence and operation of God's loving graciousness is not adequately revealed.

INDULGENCES

No way am I going to try to rehabilitate this one.

HIERARCHY

The word means either the organization of the Church in ascending grades of authority (a concept totally foreign to the gospel, though quite compatible with the platonic philosophy of the era in which the Church emerged) or the leadership of the Church (and even in the gospel the Church quite clearly has leadership). The hierarchy is a marvelous scapegoat, an inkblot on to which we can project all our frustrations, the guilty party we can blame for everything that goes wrong. Heaven knows the American hierarchy has been monumentally undistinguished in the years since the Vatican Council—perhaps less so than it has been at any time in its history. But as Eugene Kennedy has pointed out, we generally get the bishops we deserve. If the American Catholic clergy and laity are satisfied to be governed in some considerable part by mitred pinheads, then they deserve such leadership. On the other hand, it's always a lot easier to blame the hierarchy than to assume responsibility for creating renewed ideas and structures to bring new life to the Church. It is odd that often precisely those who talk most about freedom and initiative are also the ones most likely to scapegoat the hierarchy for the absence of new structures in the Church. In fact, the new Church will be built not in the chancery offices but at the grass roots, and to the extent that the new Church has failed to appear, the blame must be placed at the grass roots and not at the chanceries. It would still be nice, however, to have leaders who are intelligent, inspiring, sensitive, and sympathetic, compassionate and articulate instead of the dummies that many of us are saddled with. There are, of course, many able, intelligent, spiritually wise bishops. If you gave me some time I could maybe think of twenty.

APOSTOLIC DELEGATE

The official representative the pope sends to watch the Church in a country with which the papacy does not have diplomatic relations. (In the latter case, the same role as played by the papal nuncio, who is a formal part of the diplomatic corps.) Many Catholic observers argue that the whole concept of nuncios and delegates is outmoded in a collegial Church in which governance ought to take place under the jurisdiction of a national hierarchy. Relationships with Rome, it is said, should be channeled through the president of the hierarchy directly to Rome and not through a "foreigner" who intervenes between the pope and his brother bishops in a given country. The record of delegates and nuncios around the world at being sensitive to what is going on in many countries has not been impressive in recent years. The quality of leadership in American Catholicism declined with the appointment of Archbishop Satolli as apostolic delegate in the middle 1890s. The great episcopal leaders of the quality of John England, John Ireland, James Gibbons, John Hughes, have been few and far between since then. Apostolic delegates seem to prefer "safe" men, that is to say, mediocre non-entities with even an occasional psychopath thrown in just to spice things up a bit. Some of the recent apostolic delegates to the United States have been arrogant, insensitive, stupid, and perhaps corrupt men. The weaknesses of the system are obvious, and it must be replaced eventually. However, Paul VI clearly has no serious intention of yielding more than a few centimeters of the centralized power of the papacy. Collegiality is not operating in the Catholic Church today despite the Vatican Council. The present apostolic delegate to the United States is Jean Jadot. He is as different from his predecessors as night is from day and is almost single-handedly responsible for the tremendous change in the quality of episcopal leadership in the United States. A Jadot-like delegate—sensitive, discreet, encouraging liaison man—might prove extremely useful (perhaps with a different title) in an authentically collegial church.

HOLY DAYS OF OBLIGATION

A number of days during the year on which Catholics are supposed to go to mass. Since it turns out that it wasn't a mortal sin after all to miss mass on Sunday, *a fortiori,* it is not a mortal sin to miss mass on holy days of obligation. The original purpose of such holy days was to protect agricultural serfs from exploitation by providing them with many days when they would not be required to work. *De facto,* however, in the United States today the holy days of obligation make things more difficult for the ordinary Catholic working person who must combine church attendance with all the other responsibilities of his daily existence. The national culture has produced its own set of holy days—Fourth of July, Labor Day, Memorial Day, Thanksgiving, and, of course, Christmas (both a sacred and secular feast) on which people are free from work and for which there is an increasing custom among Catholics to attend church. An imaginative liturgical program would be more concerned about emphasizing the religious dimension of these cultural feasts (and all of them have a strong religious dimension) than about imposing obligations for feasts which are no longer culturally relevant. Such feasts as Lady Day in Harvesttime, for example, (one rich in potential symbolic impact) could easily be transferred to the nearest Sunday. The real art of liturgical innovation is not to oppose sacred holidays to secular ones but rather to integrate religion into cultural feasts. Let's see what you can do with Columbus Day, folks! I hereby propose St. Patrick's Day as the national and secular Feast of Ethnic Diversity (which, incidentally, it already is).

STERILIZATION

An increasingly popular form of birth control, especially among men. It is technically forbidden by the Church, but this prohibition seems, like all related birth control prohibitions, less and less relevant to large numbers of Catholics. Rome recently announced that prior sterilization was no longer a barrier to a valid marriage. The objection to sterilization in Catholic moral theory is that it is both a form of self-mutilation and a form of birth control. Some moral theologians seem to dissent from the notion that a vasectomy is indeed self-mutilation. I must confess that I don't feel competent about such issues, but I wonder why the self-mutilation concept is not pushed by the Roman moralists to cover other issues such as cigarette smoking and obesity.

CLERICAL GARB

Huh?

For a long time in the Church there was no distinctive clerical garb. The cassock was nothing more than a medieval scholar's gown and was worn to indicate not that you were a clergyman but that you were a scholar. Black became fashionable as part of the morbid medieval Christian belief that one should go through life wearing one's shroud as a preparation for death. If there is to be "proper" clerical garb at all, it should be joyous, celebratory, happy dress and not the grim, bizarre, distorting clothing that priests and nuns used to affect. Having said all of these things, it must still be noted that for large numbers of people, Catholic as well as non-Catholic, clerical dress was some kind of a sign—however inadequate it may have been. The religious orders of men did themselves a very great disservice by giving up that sign without finding another to replace it. The argument one heard frequently on university campuses in the 1960s from priests and nuns that religious garb was a barrier to communication with other students was malarky—though devoutly believed. The religious garb indeed marks one as different, but different/interesting for more people than different/objectionable. The solution for both priests and religious is not to go back to morose, medieval wear, nor to prance around in hippy garb, but rather to appear serenely and calmly marked as one caught up in the joyous mystery of God's presence in the world.

PIUS XII

I suppose the issue here is that Pius XII was not vigorous enough in condemning the Nazi persecution of the Jews and, indeed, was all too ready to deal with Hitler and Mussolini. Curiously enough, this attitude toward Pius XII is not based on any serious historical scholarship but rather on a German play called *The Deputy*. Why people turn to drama for serious evaluations of the papacy is an intriguing question— until one realizes how powerful anti-Catholic sentiment is in American society. Pius XII, like Pius XI before him, was committed to dealing with whatever government it was necessary to deal with to gain some margin of freedom for religious practice for Catholics. If they were not able to deal with left-wing governments as easily as they were with right-wing governments, it was not because they did not try. Curiously, many of those who thought it was wrong for the Piuses to deal with Hitler and Mussolini rejoiced when John XXIII received Krushchev's relatives and when Paul VI tried to deal with the oppressive communist governments in eastern Europe. If the Catholic Church is to deal only with democratic regimes which respect human liberties, it will not deal with many governments at all (not all that bad an idea, perhaps). As for Pius XII and the Jews, it seems to me that the overwhelming burden of serious historical research done on the subject is that his decision was arguably the right one, that any more public pronouncements on his part would have made matters worse instead of better. It is the wisdom of hindsight to say that he should have taken a more open and vigorous stance on the holocaust. Maybe he should have, but if such a stand made the holocaust worse, he would have been blamed for that too. The only kind of criticism that has any validity must take into account the ambiguity and complexities of the situation in which he found himself and concedes that in such circumstances dedicated men of good faith and good will could have arrived at very different answers without ever being sure that another answer would not have been better.

CAPITAL PUNISHMENT

Catholic moral theory has had little trouble with capital punishment until recently. Now opposition to capital punishment is the party line of liberal Catholics. The American public, however, including its Catholic component, once sympathetic to the abolition of it, has turned more and more in favor of it, believing, perhaps erroneously, that the abolition of capital punishment is somehow linked to the increase of crimes of violence (perhaps suspecting that an executed killer is much to be preferred to one who is sentenced to life imprisonment and back on the streets in five years). The present writer personally finds capital punishment extremely distasteful and would tend to be against it. But the issue is not simple; the data are inconclusive, and the attempts of liberal Catholics to equate the Catholic position with opposition to capital punishment is unjustified. Surely, in the present stage of the Church, there is room for Catholics to take divergent viewpoints on such subjects. No purpose is served by equating one particular viewpoint with the Church's stand (as the new Catechetical Directory tends to do).

CLERICALISM

Strictly speaking, clericalism is the domination by the clergy of political life. In a broader sense, clericalism is the existence of a clerical status that is sharply distinct from the lay status in the Church and claiming superior rights and arguing, *de facto* if not *de jure,* its competence to dominate everything in church life. There are some interesting twists to clericalism. For example, those who would be most opposed to the hierarchy's intervening, let us say, in an election or the abortion issue were also the ones most vigorously demanding that the hierarchy intervene to end the war in Vietnam. It seems to me you can't have it both ways; you can't insist that the hierarchy intervene in the political process selectively on your side of the question while refusing to intervene on the other side. Nor can it be, as a number of American columnists and editorial writers would apparently like to have it, that it is all right for Protestant and Jewish clergy to intervene in favor of abortion but inappropriate for Catholic clergy to intervene against it. And why is it all right for Jewish leaders to see a president about Israel and not all right for Catholics to see a president about abortion? It is also interesting to observe that many of those who are enthusiastic about Congressman Drinan were much less so about presidential speechwriter McLaughlin. It was all right, you see, for a priest to prosecute Nixon but not all right for one to defend him. The clergy should leave things to the laity except, it would seem, when their intervention is favorable to your cause. They should stay out of revolutionary movements in Northern Ireland but they're heros if they die in guerilla warfare in Latin America. Most of this is hypocritical baloney. It seems to me that John Carroll, the first American bishop, was right when he urged the clergy to stay out of party politics. The Catholic Action approach of the 1940s and 1950s was also right when it said that it was the role of the clergy to provide training and the resources of support and renewal for laity involvement in the temporal order. I argue this position not as an absolute one but rather as an ecclesiastical clerical "restraint" parallel to judicial restraint (which we don't see much of any more from the federal judiciary either). It is, finally, also interesting to note that the most liberal of clergy when they get into positions of authority seem to become authoritarian liberals all too frequently, dedicated to imposing their own policies on the laity—for their own good, of course. I am reminded of J. F. Power's classic definition of a curate as a mouse in training to be a rat.

RELICS

If relics are your thing, fine. I find the whole business creepy and possibly corrupt. But it is certainly a legitimate form of Catholic devotion. We can do without devotion to relics, but it goes back a long time—to the custom of saying mass in the tombs of martyrs and the catacombs on feast days. There is no particular reason why we need to do without it. If it offends you, forget it; if you like it, *de gustibus non est disputandum.*

FREEMASONRY

At one time the Freemasons were pagan deists, vehemently anti-Catholic, and, indeed, anti-Christian (see Mozart's *Magic Flute,* for example). In Latin countries in particular, Freemasonry was strongly tied to vicious anti-Catholicism and anticlericalism. The American masonic organizations are little more than social clubs with a lot of mumbo jumbo and bizarre garb attached. There may be still some anti-Catholic nativism in the Masons in some places not so much because they're Masons but because they are part of residual nativism in American life. Doubtless in some places, Masons may be leaning over backwards in order to be helpful to one another in the world of business and the professions (something that fortunately does not happen among Catholic ethnic groups!). It seems to be the general opinion that in most Masonic lodges, however, there is nothing objectionable to Catholics either in theory or in practice any longer.

EVIL AND SUFFERING

There is unquestionably evil in the world. It is the ultimate evil that we all must die. Why does evil exist? Why does war rage in the human condition and within our own souls? These are unanswerable questions. We simply do not know. It is difficult, of course, to see how there could be human freedom without acknowledging the human capacity for moral evil, but much of the evil in the world is caused by physical forces; the evil that flows from human actions is often greatly disproportionate to the malice of the actors involved. The critical religious question is how one can reconcile the existence of evil with the claim of an all-loving God. Bluntly spoken, how can God love us if he lets us die? Process theology solves the dilemma by deftly taking the problem out of God's hands and seeing God growing and developing through the "free" activities of his creatures. (And the process thinkers can see freedom in natural forces.) It is an interesting solution, though one not without problems of its own. (Process thinkers argue that the capacity to grow and develop is a perfection rather than an imperfection—differing in this respect from traditional Thomist notions about the attributes of God.) While the process solution may be philosophically valid, the problem still remains: How come we suffer? However, the "problem" of evil is an exclamation of confusion and protest and not a valid "argument" against goodness. To say that one cannot possibly understand how good and evil can coexist is simply to say that one cannot understand the way things really are. One no more solves that lack of understanding by denying the existence of good than one does by denying the existence of evil. The critical question is not the problem of evil and good but which way things ultimately tilt when good and evil are put together on the balance. On this matter the empirical evidence is inconclusive and one must make a leap of faith—though there is a powerful, primordial, and apparently uneradicable strain in the human personality in the direction of hopefulness.

COMMUNISM

A political system allegedly derived from the thinking of Karl Marx which purports to encompass a total philosophy of economics and administrative theory which can remake human nature, rebuild social structures, and eventually will enable men and women to live together generously and freely in economic affluence. In virtually every place in the world in which it has come to power, however, communism has turned out to be a nasty, oppressive, bureaucratic police state in which the power that claims to be the vanguard of the people has as its principal goal the continuation of its own power. It achieves that goal by total domination of all aspects of life and by the manipulation and oppression of all its citizenry. Communism is, as one of the new French left-wing philosophers has suggested, "Barbarism with a human face." And socialism (as opposed to social democracy) is little more than watered-down communism—at least in those countries where socialists have managed to take unchallenged political power. The argument that many good liberals use in favor of communism (including good Catholic liberals) is that however authoritarian and oppressive they may be, communist regimes are a way for poor countries to make dramatic economic progress. But this argument is dubious. The democratic Republic of Ireland has made far more progress than the communist People's Republic of Poland. Noncommunist Chinese regimes, such as

Taiwan, Singapore, and Hong Kong, have made far greater progress than mainland China. Costa Rica is in every respect ahead of Cuba in economic development. The more fundamental question, however, is whether the awful oppressive tyranny of communism can be justified even in the name of economic progress. It is worth noting that communist regimes never democratize, while right-wing dictatorships often do. Spain and Portugal have become democratic countires; Poland and Yugoslavia—two of the most free so-called socialist states—have not and probably will not ever (short of violent revolution) become democratic. Much of the Catholic opposition to communism in the past has been based on the notion that it is "Godless." Godless it surely is, though much of capitalism is too; a much more effective argument would be that communism is inhuman, though given the domination of the intellectual life of much of the world by watered-down Marxism, this would be a hard idea to sell. Interestingly enough, French intellectuals seem to be leading a turn away from Marxism (just at the time when a certain segment of the American Catholic elite seems to find socialism attractive).

FEMINISM

John XXIII endorsed feminism in one of his social encyclicals, but this has not changed the thinking of large numbers of churchpersons on the role of women. Nor has it led the Church in practice to turn the governance of women religious over to women. The history of Christianity has been marked by considerable ambivalence on the subject of women. Certainly in the early Church women seem to have had far more freedom and power than they did in pagan institutions. In the Middle Ages women presided over monasteries, ruled counties, assigned parish priests, gave confessional jurisdiction, and probably had more power in general than they had in any era before or since. It is also true that women religious in the United States have more check-signing power than women do in any other corporate institution. On the other hand, nuns have often been treated like second-class citizens, have been dominated by priests (and often inept priests at that), and have been excluded from policy-making roles in the Church. The Church's history, in other words, on the subject of women is complex. We have much to be ashamed of in our treatment of women; we also have a record that is better than that of most human institutions. The position on the ordination of women is allegedly based on the symbolism of the Eucharist, but the argument does not seem inherently persuasive. If anything, the Eucharist as a sacrament of nourishment might as well be maternal as paternal. Until the Holy Office statement on the ordination of women, only somewhat less than one-third of American Catholics supported it. But in the months immediately after the statement was issued, support moved up to almost one-half. One of the reasons for

Roman opposition to ordination of women is fear of offending the Orthodox churches; Rome, oddly enough, is much more afraid of offending the Orthodox than it is of offending the Anglicans. Women will eventually be ordained in the Catholic Church, I suspect, but it may take several more decades. In the meantime the Church continues to miss many opportunities to provide illumination and direction for those women who value marriage, family, and motherhood yet do not want their life energies to be completely directed to gender-linked roles. Some people articulate a reactionary and patronizing approach to women, others preach militant feminism, which in its own way is equally as patronizing. For the vast middle majority the Church does not have much to say. In some sense the ordination of women controversy has distracted the Church from this broader question. To put the matter in proper perspective, as is mentioned elsewhere in this book, the average woman at one time needed ten pregnancies to reproduce herself and would very likely be dead before her childbearing years were over. (Lucrezia Borgia died at 39, giving birth to her seventh child, which was stillborn—the fourth of her children not to survive.) Today many women can have accomplished the reproduction necessary to continue the race before they are 25, with their children safely in school before they are 30. The Church simply does not seem able to grasp the importance of this profound demographic change.

REAL PRESENCE

That Jesus is truly present in the Eucharist now seems to be a matter of agreement among all high church denominations. (See, for example, the consensus statement issued at the time of the Eucharistic Congress in Philadelphia in 1976.) The question of how Jesus is present is still a matter of theological agitation. "Transubstantiation" is a synonym for "real presence," but the use of the term does not commit contemporary Catholics to the theological explanation once attached to it. We believe that the bread "becomes" Jesus, "stands for" Jesus, "is" Jesus; but it is obvious that Jesus is present in the bread in a different way than he was present on the hills of Galilee when he was preaching. Theologians are wrestling with the way to explain this real presence of Jesus in the Eucharist, but only those Catholics with a high desire for self-torment will worry about the complexities of such explanations. There are much better things in religion to worry about.

Jesus identified himself with bread and wine. Christians have never doubted that Jesus was really present in the Eucharist, although some of the explanations they gave for the "how" of this presence have been deemed unacceptable as means of safeguarding the "fact" of the presence. In the first thousand years the explanations were mostly drawn from Platonic philosophy. Jesus was present in the Eucharist, St. Augustine told us (in words which would doubtless have gotten him into trouble in a later age if people were not careful to grasp his meaning properly) *per modum symboli*—in the manner of a symbol. He meant, of course, that Jesus was present in the Eucharist the way a platonic "idea" was present in a concrete particular. In a later and more Aristotelian era the word "transubstantiation" (change of substance) was used to convey the same or a similar idea. At the Council of Trent the word "transubstantiation" was used to defend the real presence of Jesus against some of the reformers who seemed not to sufficiently safeguard the fact of that reality to the Council fathers. (Whether they misunderstood what the reformers were about is another matter, one that will not be discussed here.) However, the Council certainly did not intend to define the Aristotelian philosophy or physics on which the word was based. Contemporary theologians are struggling for a new set of philosophical terms which can explain the "how" of the real presence in words which our own era can grasp. Their efforts have not yet been so successful as to permit us to include them in these short notes. However, it would be a mistake for a Christian to become so obsessed with the "how" of the real presence as to forget about the "fact"— especially the challenging implications and demands of that fact—and to ignore in his own life the "why."

ANGELS

Theologians wonder if the scriptural reference to angels requires Catholics to believe in creatures actually distinct from God, or do the angels merely stand for God's presence and activity in the world? The weight of opinion now seems to be in the latter direction. However, there is nothing to prevent us from believing in angels, and on the whole, the cosmos would probably be a much better place for their existence in it.

CREATION

In prechristian and early Christian times creation meant God's ordering of the cosmos, his defeat of the primal chaos. Only under the influence of Greek philosophy did the issue of creation *ex nihilo* (from nothing) arise. Christians must certainly believe, as the Old Testament teaches, that the world is subject to Yahweh, but there is no particular necessity for buying any particular explanation of how the universe came into being or any particular biological explanation of how the human race came into being (so long as the emergence of humankind is seen as a decisive step forward in God's overall plan). Neither the "big bang" nor "continuing creation" explanation of creation has or can have any particular theological advantage.

RELIGIOUS FREEDOM

After many alarums and excursions, advances and retreats, marches and countermarches—and a fair amount of feet-stomping by such Americans as Cardinal Meyer—the Second Vatican Council got around to acknowledging what has been true for the whole history of Christianity: the acceptance of the gospel is a matter of free choice and can be neither physically or morally constrained. Jesus made that clear, St. Paul made that clear, but a lot of Christian leaders, Catholic and non-Catholic, have forgotten it repeatedly down through the course of human history. The experience of the Americans at the Second Vatican Council (and the persecution of John Courtney Murray in the years preceding the Council) indicate how reluctant Catholic Church leadership was to acknowledge the ultimate and decisive freedom of the human religious act. Even now in many Catholic countries the Church is reluctant to give up the special position which in effect discriminates against religious freedom of choice. It is time for such obscurantist relics of past mistakes to be permanently expurgated.

CHURCH AND STATE

Whatever was to be said of the advantages of the links between church and state in bygone years—and one might be prepared to concede that in certain times and certain places it was the only meaningful option—there isn't now any solid reason for Catholicism to want to be the established church. Indeed, it is not the established church in any country, while Anglicanism is in England and Presbyterianism is in Scotland, and Lutheranism is in the Scandinavian countries. In some countries the Church enjoys the status of being noted constitutionally as the "religion of the majority of the people," which usually means that the state has the right to interfere in one way or another in the appointment of bishops—and perhaps has the obligation of pay for or to provide religious education in the public schools. In the long run the Church always seems to come out the loser when it is too closely tied up with civil authority. (The languid and passive state of the Orthodox church vis-a-vis the civil society is ample proof of such an assertion.) The sooner the Church can disengage itself from too close a tie with civil governments in the world, the better off it will be. On the other hand, the notion of a "wall of separation" between church and state in the United States (which mostly means no money for Catholic schools) is a creation of twentieth-century antireligious legal theory, to say nothing of twentieth-century anti-Catholic nativism, and has no grounds either in the Constitution or in nineteenth-century legal and civil practice.

MARY

The historic function of Mary in the Catholic tradition is to reflect the womanliness of God, just as Jesus reflects the manliness of God. Jesus and Mary together represent the fact that God is androgynous, that in God are those characteristics which we humans separate under the title of "manly" and "womanly" or "masculine" and "feminine" are combined and blended. God can just as legitimately be called "our loving mother" as "our loving father." Mary represents the Catholic Christian continuity with the maternal deities of pre-christian times, and is in fact, in this feminist age, the only woman deity in the marketplace. Mary has also been the most powerful cultural symbol in the Western world, and is greatly appreciated today by such Protestants and non-Catholic writers as Harvey Cox and Theodore Rozak, even though we Catholics seem momentarily to have lost sight of her importance. Mary is one of the most powerful un-utilized resources available to Catholic Christianity, and the refusal of Catholic elite scholars to take Mary seriously is evidence of their insensitivity and historical naivete.*

* For more on this, see Andrew M. Greeley, *The Mary Myth* (New York: Seabury Press, 1977).